SCRIPT
BRUNO CÉNOU

ILLUSTRATIONS
DAVID CÉNOU

TRANSLATED FROM THE FRENCH BY OLIVIA TAYLOR SMITH

PANTHERS
IN THE HOLE

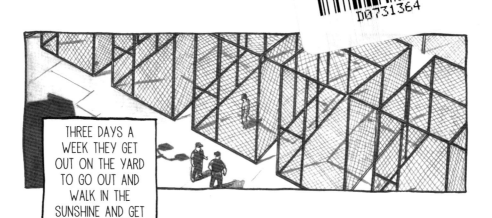

THREE DAYS A
WEEK THEY GET
OUT ON THE YARD
TO GO OUT AND
WALK IN THE
SUNSHINE AND GET
THEIR VITAMIN D...

PHONEME
MEDIA

PANTHERS
IN THE HOLE

Phoneme Media

P.O. Box 411272

Los Angeles, CA 90041

First Edition, 2016

Published by arrangement with La boîte à bulles

and in cooperation with Amnesty International.

ISBN: 978-1-939419-81-1

This book is distributed by Publishers Group West.

Printed in Canada

Lettered by Jaya Nicely

Phoneme Media is a nonprofit media company, a fiscally sponsored

project of Pen Center USA, dedicated to increasing cross-cultural understanding,

connecting people and ideas through the art of translation.

Statements by characters in this book were gathered by the authors from publicly available sources:

Civil Action No. 06-789-JJB-CN, Albert Woodfox, #72148 versus Burl Cain, et al (United States District Court, State of Louisiana October 22, 2008). Deposition of Warden Burl Cain

King, Robert Hillary. *From the Bottom of the Heap: The Autobiography of Black Panther Robert Hillary King*. Oakland, CA: PM Press, 2009.

McGaughy, Laura. "Dying Angola 3 Member Herman Wallace Reindicted, Report Says." *The Times-Picayune*, October 03, 2013. Accessed May 5, 2016. http://www.nola.com/crime/baton-rouge/index.ssf/2013/10/herman_wallace_angola_3_indict.html.

"Angola Prison: A Place of Encouragement, An Interview with Burl Cain." *Religion & Liberty* 22, no. 3 (Summer 2012). http://www.acton.org/pub/religion-liberty/volume-22-number-3/angola-prison-place-encouragement.

Ridgeway, James. "God's Own Warden." *Mother Jones*, July/August 2011. http://www.motherjones.com/politics/2011/07/burl-cain-angola-prison.

Ridgeway, James, and Jean Casella. "Louisiana Attorney General Says Angola 3 'Have Never Been Held in Solitary Confinement.'." Mother Jones. March 23, 2013. Accessed May 5, 2016. http://www.motherjones.com/politics/2013/03/louisiana-attorney-general-says-angola-3-have-never-been-held-solitary-confinement.

In the Land of the Free. Directed by Jean Vadim. 2010. DVD.

Wallace, Herman. "The Rise and Fall of the Angola Prison Chapter of the Black Panther Party." Official Website of the Black Panther Party Alumni. Accessed May 5, 2016. http://www.itsabouttimebpp.com/Political_Prisoners/pdf/The_Rise_and_Fall_of_the_Angola_Prison_Chapter_of_the_Black_Panther_Party.pdf.

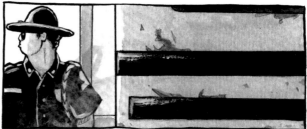

LOUISIANA STATE PENITENTIARY

LOUISIANA STATE PRISON, AKA "ANGOLA".

LOUISIANA STATE PENITENTIARY

STOP

CREATED AFTER THE CIVIL WAR,

BUILT ON FIVE
FORMER PLANTATIONS,

IT'S NAMED AFTER THE HOMELAND

OF ITS ORIGINAL
FORCED LABORERS.

THE INCARCERATED CURRENTLY
WORK FOR A SALARY OF
2 TO 20 CENTS AN HOUR.

OF THOSE 5,000 DETAINED AT ANGOLA, CLOSE TO 70% HAVE BEEN SENTENCED TO LIFE. THE CHANCES OF BEING RELEASED ON PAROLE ARE SLIM TO NONE.*

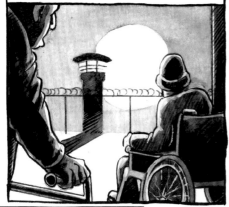

YOU GET OLD AND DIE AT ANGOLA. THE INMATES REMAIN IN THE PRISON'S HOSPICE AND PALLIATIVE CARE UNTIL THE LAST MOMENTS OF THEIR SENTENCE.**

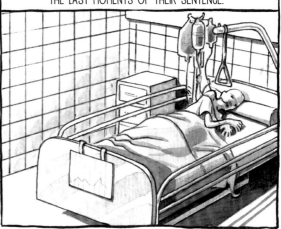

THE PRISON'S CEMETERY, POINT LOOKOUT, IS THE FINAL RESTING PLACE FOR THOSE WHOSE FAMILIES DON'T CLAIM THE BODY.

AT ANGOLA, EACH SUNDAY IN OCTOBER, WE SEE PEOPLE FROM THE OUTSIDE WHO COME AND BUY TICKETS

Will call at all windows

TICKETS   TICKETS   TICK

TO WATCH A SHOW

LOUISIANA LOTTERY   Coca-Cola

*THERE WERE FOUR RELEASES A YEAR IN 2009 – 2010.
**THIRTY INMATES DIED PER YEAR IN 2009 – 2010.

THAT STARS THE INMATES THEMSELVES: THE BIG ANGOLA RODEO.

CONVICT POKER, THE MOST POPULAR EVENT, THRILLS THE SPECTATORS WHO HAVE TRAVELED FROM AFAR TO SEE IT.

THE LAST PLAYER STILL SITTING IN HIS CHAIR WINS $200, OR IF HE'S LUCKY HE'LL BE INJURED SO BADLY THAT IT'S FATAL

AND HE COULD DIE OUTSIDE, A FREE MAN!

BURL CAIN, THE WARDEN OF ANGOLA UNTIL EARLY 2016, GUARANTEED AND ENFORCED A REHABILITATION MODEL FOUNDED ON WORK, EDUCATION,

AND THE CHRISTIAN FAITH.

AT ANGOLA, INMATES CAN LEARN TO READ,

TO REPAIR CARS,

CLANG

OR TO GROW TREES.

BUT THE ONLY COLLEGE-LEVEL COURSE THAT A SMALL NUMBER WILL TAKE

IS THE ONE ADMINISTERED BY A BAPTIST PREACHER FROM NEW ORLEANS. THE GRADUATES RECEIVE A DIPLOMA TO SERVE IN THE DENOMINATION'S MINISTRY.

IF YOU TURN TO A MORAL WORLDVIEW, YOU'LL BE OKAY. BUT IF WE TURN AWAY FROM OUR RELIGIOUS HERITAGE AND WE KEEP SEPARATION OF CHURCH AND STATE TO THE POINT THAT IS A WIDER GAP THAN OUR FOREFATHERS INTENDED, YOU'RE GOING TO KEEP HAVING IMMORAL ACTS

AND IMMORAL THINGS HAPPEN.

BURL CAIN WENT BEYOND HIS RESPONSIBILITIES AS WARDEN

AND FANCIED HIMSELF AS A SPIRITUAL FATHER...

THEY DIDN'T LISTEN TO THEIR PARENTS. THEY DIDN'T LISTEN TO LAW ENFORCEMENT. SO WHEN THEY GET HERE, I BECOME THEIR DADDY.

AND THEY WILL EITHER LISTEN TO ME

OR MAKE THEIR TIME HERE VERY HARD.

HE EXPLAINED TO STUDENTS VISITING THE PRISON.

11

ALBERT WOODFOX, HERMAN WALLACE, AND ROBERT KING, LIKE THE THOUSAND OTHER CURRENT OCCUPANTS OF THE CLOSE CELL RESTRICTED UNIT (CCR), ARE WELL ACQUAINTED WITH CAIN'S IRON-FISTED ZEALOTRY.

ALBERT WOODFOX, CONFINED IN ISOLATION AT ANGOLA FROM 1972 TO 2010, THEN HELD AT THE DAVID WADE CORRECTIONAL FACILITY, FROM WHICH HE WAS RELEASED IN EARLY 2016.

HERMAN WALLACE, CONFINED IN ISOLATION AT ANGOLA FROM 1972 TO 2009, THEN AT THE HUNT CORRECTIONAL CENTER UNTIL SEPTEMBER 2013, WAS RELEASED ON OCTOBER 1, 2013, AND PASSED AWAY JUST THREE DAYS LATER.

ROBERT KING WAS CONFINED IN ISOLATION AT ANGOLA BEGINNING IN 1972, AND RELEASED IN 2001.

IN THE CCR, YOU HAVE BOOKS TO READ, MAGAZINES TO READ IF YOU WANT. YOU HAVE A TELEVISION ON THE WALL OUTSIDE THE CELL THAT YOU CAN SEE, AND YOU CAN WITHIN REASON WATCH WHAT YOU WANT.

THEY ALL AGREE WHAT THEY'RE GOING TO WATCH

AND THEY WATCH THAT. THEY HAVE A CHOICE.

AND SO THEY CAN LIVE IN THAT—

THEY GET ONE HOUR OUT

TO BE OUT ON THE TIER.

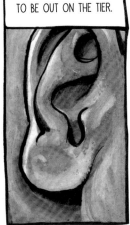

THREE DAYS A WEEK THEY GET ON THE YARD

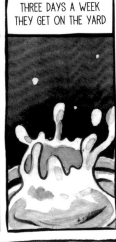

TO GO OUT AND WALK IN THE SUNSHINE

AND GET THEIR VITAMIN D AND EXERCISE ON THE YARD.

BURL CAIN HAS MADE UP HIS MIND ON ALBERT WOODFOX.

THE THING ABOUT HIM IS THAT HE WANTS TO DEMONSTRATE. HE WANTS TO ORGANIZE. HE WANTS TO BE DEFIANT. HE WANTS TO SHOW TO OTHERS THAT HE IS POWERFUL AND STRONG.

THERE IS NO SUCH THING AS A PEACEFUL DEMONSTRATION IN PRISON. YOU KNOW, WHEN YOU'RE DEMONSTRATING, YOU'RE BEING DEFIANT TO AUTHORITY...

I STILL KNOW HE HAS A PROPENSITY FOR VIOLENCE. I STILL KNOW THAT HE IS STILL TRYING TO PRACTICE BLACK PANTHERISM,

AND I STILL WOULD NOT WANT HIM WALKING AROUND MY PRISON BECAUSE HE WOULD ORGANIZE THE YOUNG NEW INMATES.

I WOULD HAVE ME ALL KIND OF PROBLEMS, MORE THAN I COULD STAND,

AND I WOULD HAVE THE BLACKS CHASING AFTER THEM. I WOULD HAVE CHAOS AND CONFLICT,

AND I BELIEVE THAT.

ROBERT KING

HEY BIG GUY, WHERE DO YOU THINK YOU'RE GOING?

NEW ORLEANS, LATE 1940S.

WHOA, HE MUST WEIGH OVER 3 POUNDS!

MAYBE NOT 3 POUNDS, BUT HE SURE LOOKS WELL FED.

AH HA HA!

MY NAME IS ROBERT HILLARY KING. I WAS BORN IN THE UNITED STATES OF AMERICA.

15

I WAS BORN BLACK.

DON'T MOVE, GUYS!

FUCK!

CORNER HIM, ASSHOLE!

SSSHHHH...SOFTLY... MY SWEET, VERRRRY SOFTLYYYY

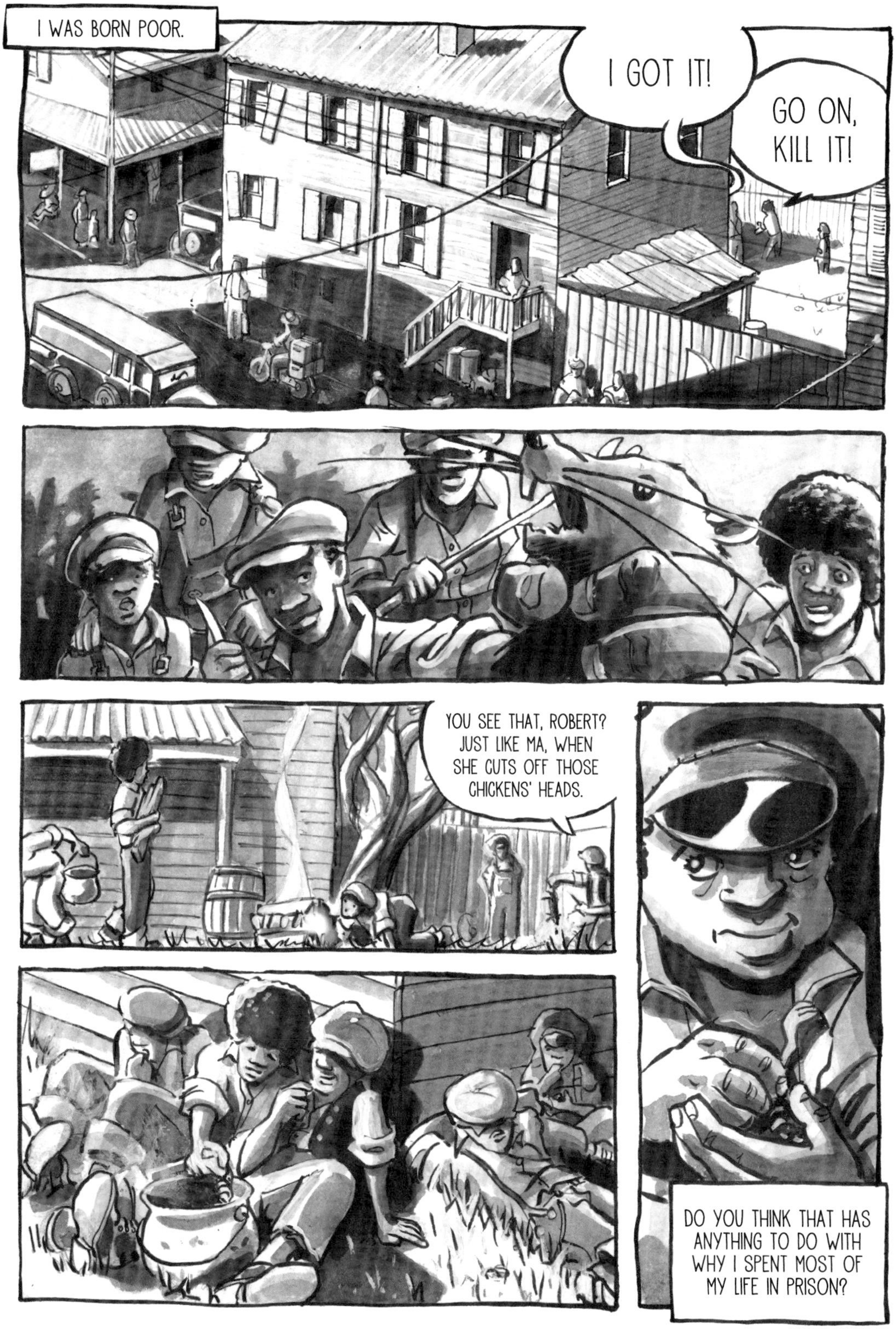
I WAS BORN POOR.
I GOT IT!
GO ON, KILL IT!
YOU SEE THAT, ROBERT? JUST LIKE MA, WHEN SHE CUTS OFF THOSE CHICKENS' HEADS.
DO YOU THINK THAT HAS ANYTHING TO DO WITH WHY I SPENT MOST OF MY LIFE IN PRISON?

NEW ORLEANS, 1961.

HEY, ROBERT... SEE THAT GUY DOWN THERE?

HE LOOKS...

...TOTALLY LOADED!

COME ON, PULL OVER! WE CAN'T LEAVE HIM LIKE THIS!

ALRIGHT, FINE. CALM DOWN!

OK, LET'S CHECK IT OUT. GUYS?

OKAY.

HEY! NEED A HAND, SIR?

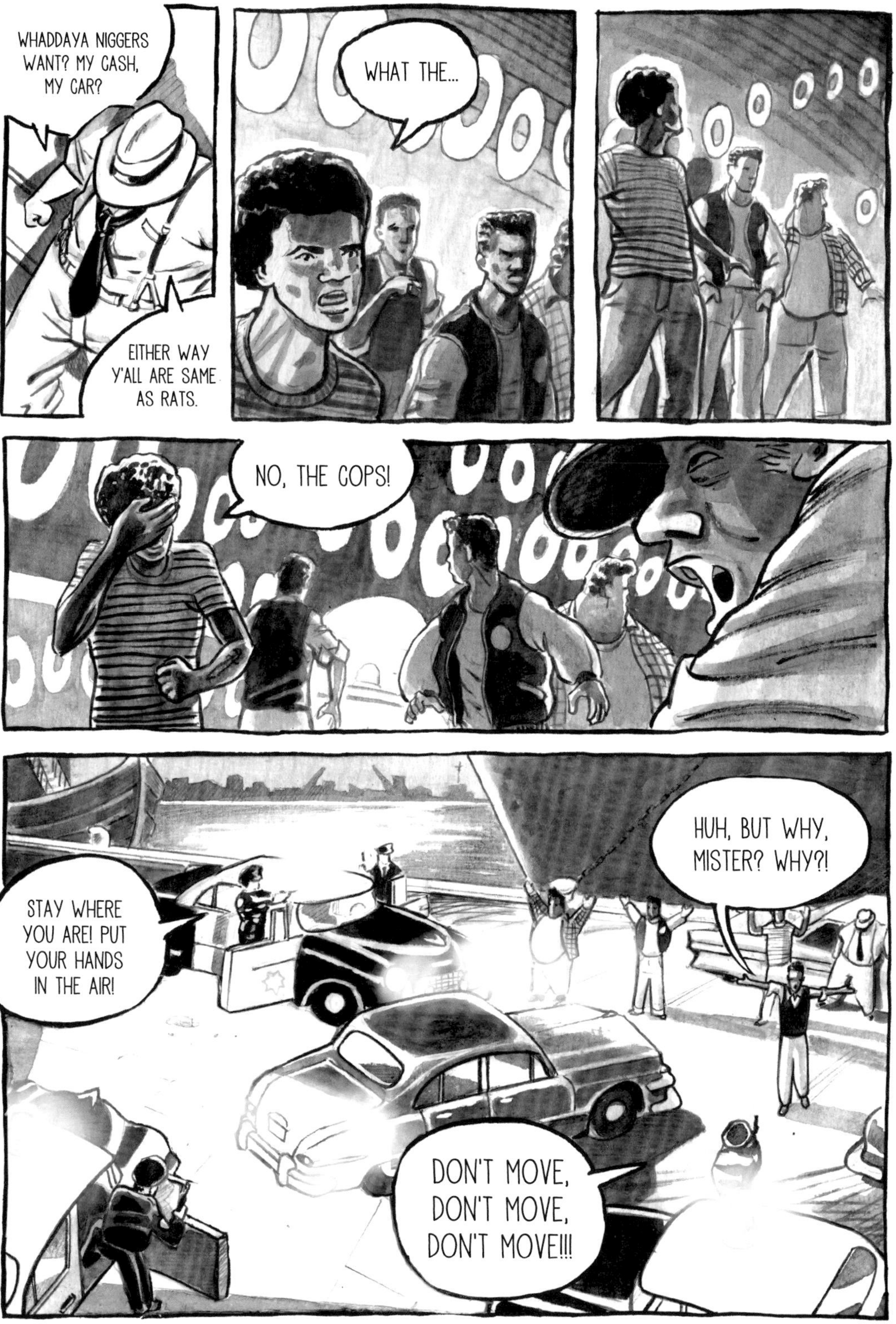
WHADDAYA NIGGERS WANT? MY CASH, MY CAR?
EITHER WAY Y'ALL ARE SAME AS RATS.
WHAT THE...
NO, THE COPS!
HUH, BUT WHY, MISTER? WHY?!
STAY WHERE YOU ARE! PUT YOUR HANDS IN THE AIR!
DON'T MOVE, DON'T MOVE, DON'T MOVE!!!

THE POLICE HAD A SPECIAL WAY OF CLEARING OUT THEIR PAPER WORK: IF A CRIME WENT UNSOLVED, THEY WOULD ARREST A NEGRO, PREFERABLY A YOUNG ONE WITH A RECORD, ACCUSE THEM, BEAT THEM, AND FORCE THEM TO CONFESS.

THIS TIME THE COPS FOUND THAT MY FRIENDS AND I FIT THE DESCRIPTION OF SUSPECTS CONNECTED TO A RECENT STRING OF ROBBERIES.

AND THE ALLEGED VICTIMS CONFIRMED THIS LUCKY GUESS.

WHEN IT CAME TO ME, I HADN'T BEEN RECOGNIZED, BUT SINCE I'D BEEN ARRESTED WITH THE OTHERS, I MUST HAVE BEEN GUILTY OF SOMETHING. I WAS ACCUSED OF BEING THE GROUP'S DRIVER, EVEN THOUGH AT THE TIME, I HAD NEVER EVEN TOUCHED A STEERING WHEEL.

SOMETHING ANY SERIOUS LAWYER, OR EVEN JUST A PAID ONE, COULD HAVE EASILY PROVEN.

WE LEARNED THAT THE DRUNK WE'D WORRIED ABOUT HAD BEEN ARRESTED FOR DRIVING WHILE LIQUORED UP AND WAS PLANTED THERE AS BAIT. WE HAD SIMPLY BEEN TRICKED.

NEXT TIME, IT'LL BE THE JUDGE!

AT YOUR SERVICE, SIR.

SCRAM!

IN 1961, THE MAXIMUM SENTENCE FOR ARMED ROBBERY WAS 30 YEARS.*

YOUR LAWYERS ARE HERE!

*SINCE THEN, SENTENCES OF OVER 100 YEARS HAVE BEEN HANDED OUT FOR SIMILAR CHARGES IN LOUISIANA.

OUR OFFICIALLY ASSIGNED LAWYERS CONVINCED US TO AVOID THE TRIAL. ACCORDING TO THEM, THE ATTORNEY GENERAL WOULD NOT SPARE US, AND IT HAD ALREADY BEEN DECIDED THAT WE WOULD GET THE MAXIMUM. WE FELT THE PRESSURE SO WE TOOK THE PLEA DEAL FOR JUST TEN YEARS DOING HARD LABOR, WHICH WE HAD TO DO AT THE LOUISIANA STATE PENITENTIARY.

YOU WANT TO MAKE AN APPEAL? HUH, WHAT ARE YOU SAYING?

YOU ARE YOUNG. YOU HAVE YOUR WHOLE LIFE AHEAD OF YOU!

YOU'LL SEE, YOU WILL THANK ME ONE DAY, KID!!!

PRAY, KEEP THE FAITH!

MY PROMOTION WAS QUICK: IN JUST A FEW MONTHS I WENT FROM THE CORRECTIONAL FACILITY FOR JUVENILE DELINQUENTS TO PRISON FOR ADULTS. I WASN'T AN ANGEL. I HAD COMMITTED BURGLARIES, STOLEN FROM BODEGAS, BUT I CAN TELL YOU THAT EVERY TIME I WAS ARRESTED AND SENT TO PRISON IT WAS FOR SOMETHING I DIDN'T DO. I'VE NEVER BEEN ARRESTED FOR WHAT I'VE REALLY DONE.

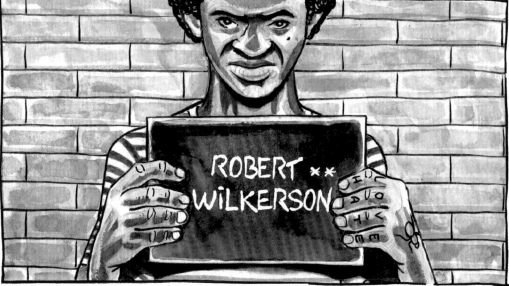

**ROBERT WILKERSON CHANGED HIS NAME TO "ROBERT HILLARY KING" AFTER HIS RELEASE.

GENTLEMEN, WELCOME TO ANGOLA!

I WAS TERRIFIED.

WE WERE FRESH MEAT. I QUICKLY LEARNED THAT PROSTITUTION WAS NOT ONLY TOLERATED

BUT ENCOURAGED BY THE GUARDS,

WHO PROFITED FROM IT.

NEWCOMERS HAD TO PROVE THAT THEY WERE TOUGH RIGHT AWAY

OTHERWISE THEY WOULD BE RAPED.

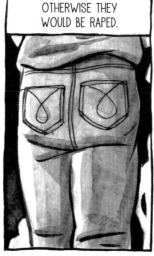

SOME DIED, OTHERS WERE FORCED TO LIVE AS SEX SLAVES

FOR 10, 15, 20 YEARS.

I IMMEDIATELY UNDERSTOOD THAT EVERYTHING HERE REVOLVED AROUND HARD LABOR:
WORK WAS THE PRISON'S LEITMOTIF, ITS GUIDING PRINCIPLE.

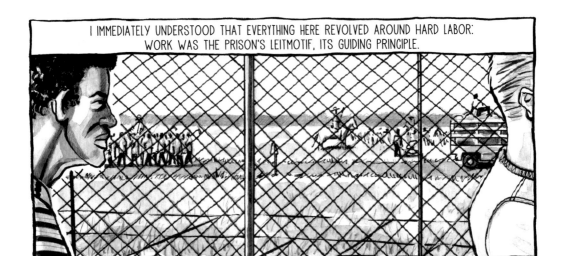

LIKE THE GUARDS SAID, "IF YOU'VE
GOT A PAIR, YOU GOTTA WORK."

EXCEPT FOR THOSE SHUT FOR 23 HOURS A DAY IN
ISOLATION FOR SECURITY REASONS. THEY WERE DEPRIVED OF
THE OPPORTUNITY TO MAKE 2-AND-A-HALF CENTS AN HOUR.

AT ANGOLA, EVEN AFTER 1960, SEGREGATION REIGNED, BUT THERE WAS A MORE INSIDIOUS
DIVISION AT THE HEART OF THE PRISON POPULATION. ARMED WITH GUNS FURNISHED BY THE
STATE OF LOUISIANA, "TRUSTEES" WERE CHARGED WITH MAINTAINING ORDER IN THE PRISON.

THESE CONDEMNED KHAKI—WEARING MEN WERE THE DORSAL SPINE OF THE ENTIRE PRISON. NEARLY 90% OF SECURITY RESTED ON THEIR SHOULDERS AND THEIR EGOS. THEY TOOK ON THIS RESPONSIBILITY LIKE A PACK OF RABID, WELL—TRAINED DOGS, AS THOUGH THEIR LIVES DEPENDED ON IT. THEY FOLLOWED THE GUARDS' ORDERS, REASSURING THE GUARDS IN THE OBSERVATION TOWERS, SURVEYING THE WORK TEAMS AND HELPING THEMSELVES TO THE UNDERGROUND TOBACCO TRADE, WHICH THEY OFTEN CONTROLLED. WHEN A HOPELESS MAN TRIED TO ESCAPE, THEY WOULD LEAD THE HUNT. THEY ESSENTIALLY RULED THE PRISON, AND ALMOST EVERYONE HELD THE GUARDS AND THOSE FELLOW INMATES IN EQUAL CONTEMPT.

IT WAS THE FALL OF 1961, AND I WAS 18. I CAME TO ANGOLA PROUD, CONFIDENT IN MYSELF AND RESOLUTE, UNCONCERNED WITH MY OWN ACTIONS AND BEHAVIOR.

I LATER UNDERSTOOD, WITH THE HELP OF MY UNCLE HENRY WHO WAS ALSO AT ANGOLA AT THE TIME, THAT THIS ATTITUDE WAS SUICIDAL. THIS WAS A PLACE AT WAR, WHERE THE YOUTH OF THE BLACK NATION WAS IMPLODING, KILLING ITSELF FROM WITHIN OVER TRIVIALITIES AND RELISHING IN SPILLING ITS OWN BLOOD.

I LEARNED TO BLEND IN WITH THE HERD. I READ A LOT, ESPECIALLY THE BIBLE. I LEARNED TO BOX AND I SURVIVED.

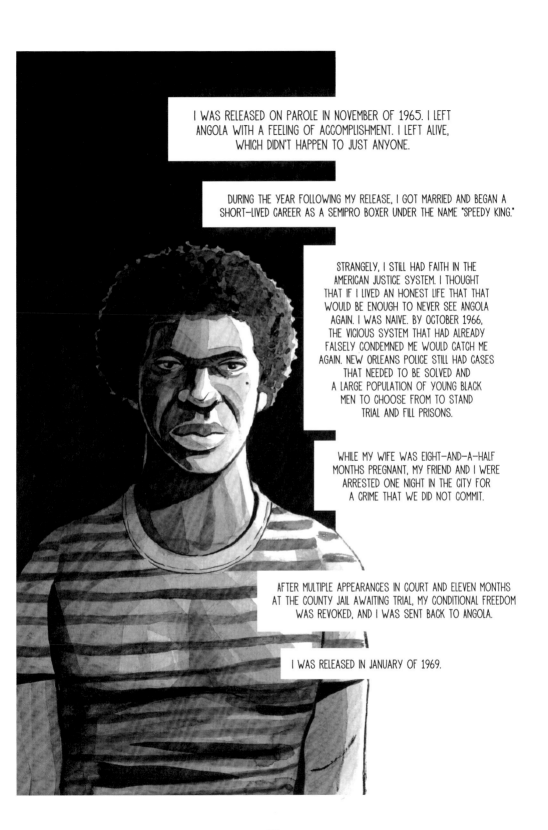

I WAS RELEASED ON PAROLE IN NOVEMBER OF 1965. I LEFT ANGOLA WITH A FEELING OF ACCOMPLISHMENT. I LEFT ALIVE, WHICH DIDN'T HAPPEN TO JUST ANYONE.

DURING THE YEAR FOLLOWING MY RELEASE, I GOT MARRIED AND BEGAN A SHORT-LIVED CAREER AS A SEMIPRO BOXER UNDER THE NAME "SPEEDY KING."

STRANGELY, I STILL HAD FAITH IN THE AMERICAN JUSTICE SYSTEM. I THOUGHT THAT IF I LIVED AN HONEST LIFE THAT THAT WOULD BE ENOUGH TO NEVER SEE ANGOLA AGAIN. I WAS NAIVE. BY OCTOBER 1966, THE VICIOUS SYSTEM THAT HAD ALREADY FALSELY CONDEMNED ME WOULD CATCH ME AGAIN. NEW ORLEANS POLICE STILL HAD CASES THAT NEEDED TO BE SOLVED AND A LARGE POPULATION OF YOUNG BLACK MEN TO CHOOSE FROM TO STAND TRIAL AND FILL PRISONS.

WHILE MY WIFE WAS EIGHT-AND-A-HALF MONTHS PREGNANT, MY FRIEND AND I WERE ARRESTED ONE NIGHT IN THE CITY FOR A CRIME THAT WE DID NOT COMMIT.

AFTER MULTIPLE APPEARANCES IN COURT AND ELEVEN MONTHS AT THE COUNTY JAIL AWAITING TRIAL, MY CONDITIONAL FREEDOM WAS REVOKED, AND I WAS SENT BACK TO ANGOLA.

I WAS RELEASED IN JANUARY OF 1969.

27

EARLY MARCH, 1970. DETECTIVES ARRIVED AT MY HOME WITHOUT A WARRANT, SEARCHED MY HOUSE AND TURNED IT INSIDE OUT, NATURALLY FINDING THE GUN THAT THEY HAD COME TO FIND. I LEARNED THAT AN ARMED ROBBERY HAD BEEN COMMITTED BY TWO MEN, ONE OF WHOM WAS IDENTIFIED AND ARRESTED, AND HE HAD NAMED ME AS HIS ACCOMPLICE.

A JOKE OF A TRIAL TOOK PLACE. IN THE EARLY DEPOSITIONS, VICTIMS DESCRIBED A MAN AROUND 40 YEARS OLD, WHILE I WAS ONLY 26 AND LOOKED 20. EITHER WAY, I WAS FOUND GUILTY AND SENTENCED TO 35 YEARS.

IT NO LONGER MATTERED TO ME. MY LAWYER FILED AN APPEAL, BUT I DIDN'T CARE.

I UNDERSTOOD THAT TRUTH AND EQUALITY HAD NO PLACE IN THIS STORY. I FELT COMPLETELY FREE OF ANY MORAL RESPECT FOR THE SYSTEM AND DECIDED TO ESCAPE. WITH 20 OTHER PRISONERS, WE BUSTED OUT OF THE COUNTY JAIL. ONLY THREE OF US WOULD SUCCEED. I WAS ONE OF THEM.

I WAS FOUND TWO WEEKS LATER AND SLAPPED WITH AN EXTRA 8 YEARS FOR AGGRAVATED ASSAULT.

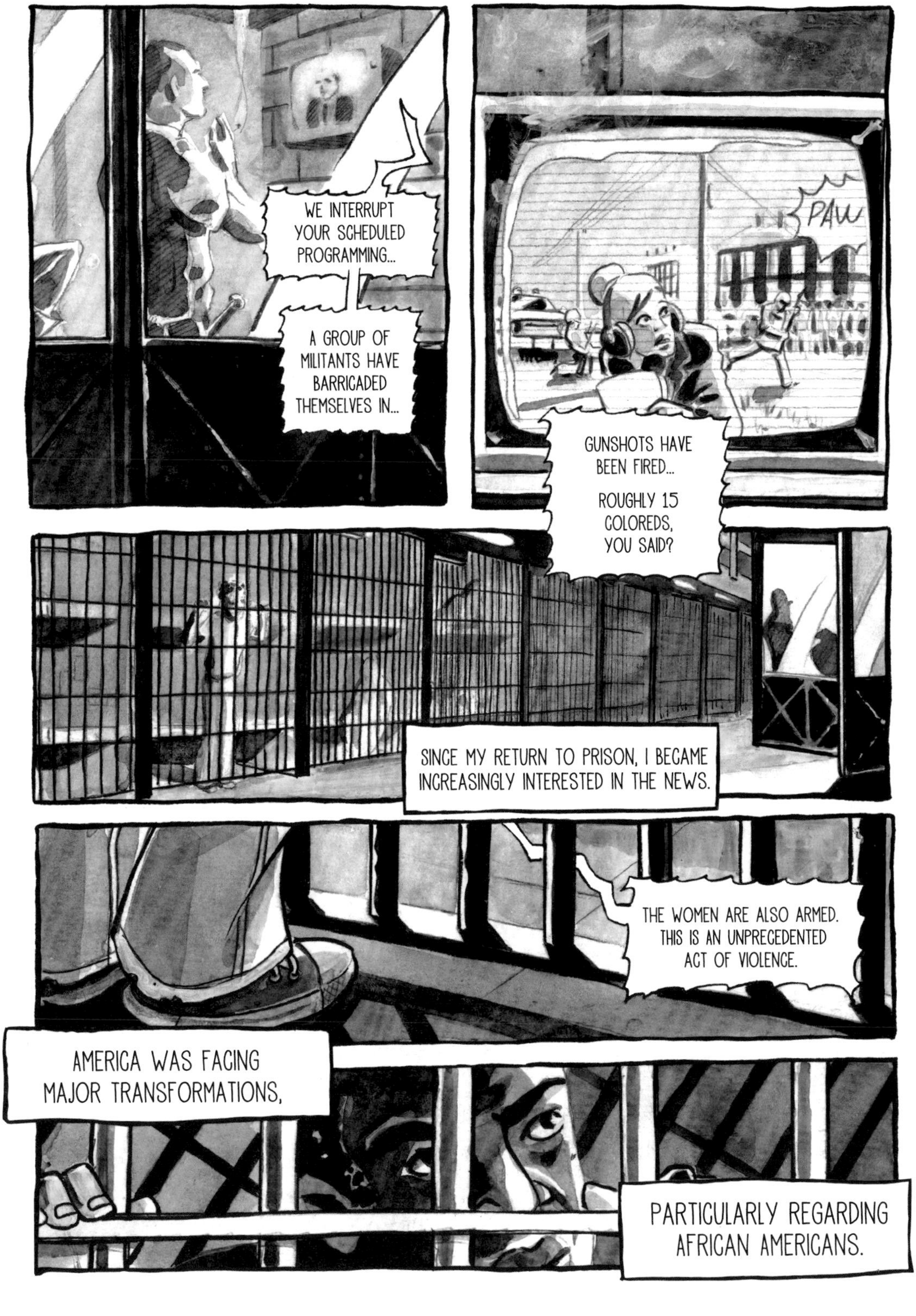
WE INTERRUPT YOUR SCHEDULED PROGRAMMING...
A GROUP OF MILITANTS HAVE BARRICADED THEMSELVES IN...
PAW
GUNSHOTS HAVE BEEN FIRED...
ROUGHLY 15 COLOREDS, YOU SAID?
SINCE MY RETURN TO PRISON, I BECAME INCREASINGLY INTERESTED IN THE NEWS.
THE WOMEN ARE ALSO ARMED. THIS IS AN UNPRECEDENTED ACT OF VIOLENCE.
AMERICA WAS FACING MAJOR TRANSFORMATIONS,
PARTICULARLY REGARDING AFRICAN AMERICANS.

SEPTEMBER 15TH, 1970. PIETY ST., IN THE LOWER NINTH WARD* OF NEW ORLEANS.

PAW

PAW

HEY, DO YOU KNOW WHAT WE'RE SHOOTING AT, BOYS?!

DON'T WORRY, JUST A BUNCH OF NIGGERS!

ON THIS DAY, THE AUTHORITIES DECIDED TO PUT AN END TO THE LOCAL LOUISIANA CHAPTER OF THE BLACK PANTHERS, A NEWLY FORMED POLITICAL PARTY THAT WAS TRYING TO REBUILD A NEIGHBORHOOD THAT HAD BEEN ABANDONED TO VIOLENCE AND POVERTY.

*THE LOWER NINTH WARD WAS AN IMPOVERISHED NEIGHBORHOOD ON THE EAST SIDE OF NEW ORLEANS, BORDERED ON THE SOUTH BY THE MISSISSIPPI, AND AT THE NORTH BY THE INDUSTRIAL CANAL, AND ALMOST ENTIRELY DESTROYED BY HURRICANE KATRINA IN 2005.

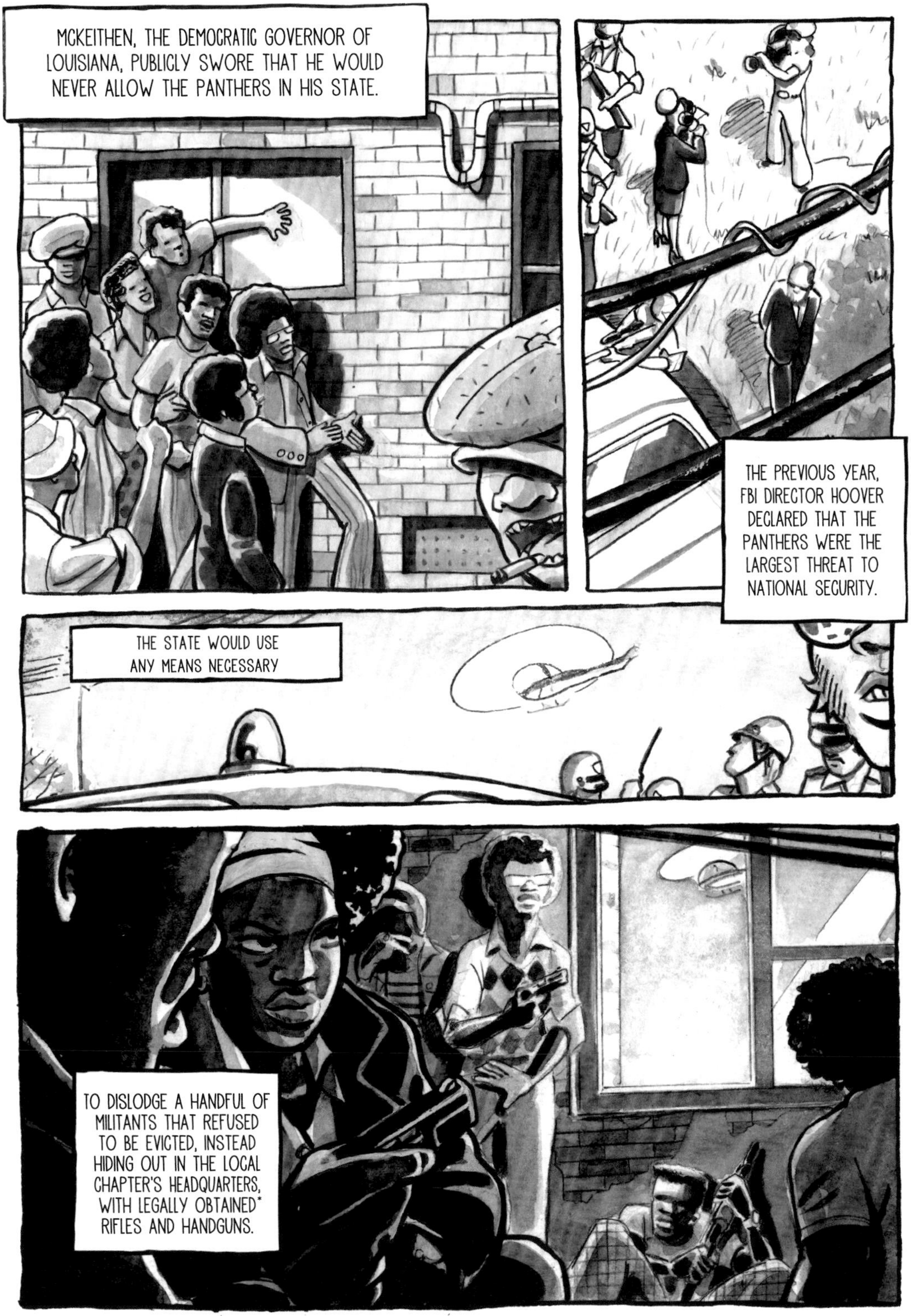
MCKEITHEN, THE DEMOCRATIC GOVERNOR OF LOUISIANA, PUBLICLY SWORE THAT HE WOULD NEVER ALLOW THE PANTHERS IN HIS STATE.
THE PREVIOUS YEAR, FBI DIRECTOR HOOVER DECLARED THAT THE PANTHERS WERE THE LARGEST THREAT TO NATIONAL SECURITY.
THE STATE WOULD USE ANY MEANS NECESSARY
TO DISLODGE A HANDFUL OF MILITANTS THAT REFUSED TO BE EVICTED, INSTEAD HIDING OUT IN THE LOCAL CHAPTER'S HEADQUARTERS, WITH LEGALLY OBTAINED* RIFLES AND HANDGUNS.

*ONE OF THE PARTY'S PRINCIPLES IS COMMUNITY SELF-DEFENSE. SINCE THE POLICE FORCE DID NOT PROTECT OR SERVE BLACK POPULATIONS, THE PARTY REQUIRED MEANS OF MAINTAINING SECURITY, ALL WHILE STAYING WITHIN THE LAW AND PROTECTED BY THE 2ND AMENDMENT.

THERE WERE 12 OF THEM, 9 MEN AND 3 WOMEN, ALL LESS THAN 23 YEARS OLD. THEY ALL CAME OUT UNINJURED, DESPITE THE POLICE'S AGGRESSIVE GUN USE. THEY WERE ALL ARRESTED AND ACCUSED OF ATTEMPTED MURDER AND CRIMINAL TRESPASSING.

THEY WERE INCARCERATED AT THE COUNTY JAIL, WHERE I WAS ABLE TO MEET MOST OF THEM. THEY EXPLAINED PART OF THEIR AGENDA TO ME AND MADE ME AWARE OF THE OPPRESSION EXERTED BY THE UNITED STATES ON THE BLACK COMMUNITY AND THE DISENFRANCHISED IN GENERAL.

THEY TAUGHT ME THE POWER OF COMMUNITY AND THE MEANS AND METHODS OF THE POLITICAL STRUGGLE.

HERMAN WALLACE

JANUARY 13TH, 1967.

C'MON JOHN, LET'S GO!

YEEHAW!

TWO DAYS LATER.

HERMAN, LET'S GO TO BED, IT'S ALREADY 5 IN THE MORNING!

THIS ASSHOLE ISN'T GOING TO BED BEFORE HE CLEANS US ALL OUT!

THE COPS BUSTED IN EARLY THAT SUNDAY MORNING.

I WAS 25 YEARS OLD. I WAS HANDSOME, I WAS STRONG, I WAS REALLY STUPID. I WAS JUST SOME PUNK, BUT I WANTED TO MAKE A NAME FOR MYSELF. MY PALS AND I HAD DONE SOME PETTY CRIMES, BUT THAT DAY WE DECIDED TO KNOCK OVER A NATIONAL BANK IN THE MIDDLE OF NEW ORLEANS. WE LEFT WITH $60,000. WE WERE FINALLY RESPECTABLE BANK ROBBERS.

WE WERE SENTENCED TO 50 YEARS HARD LABOR.

I ESCAPED DURING THE TRIAL. I WAS DRIVEN ALL THE WAY TO PENSACOLA, FLORIDA.

HERMAN WALLACE

I WAS ARRESTED THERE THREE YEARS LATER

AND BROUGHT BACK TO JAIL IN NEW ORLEANS.*

WELCOME TO THE C1, BROTHER. YOU KNOW THIS IS THE PANTHERS' ROW?

THAT'S WHAT THEY SAID. I DON'T KNOW WHAT I'M DOING HERE.

* THE COUNTY JAIL WHERE KING WAS ALSO INCARCERATED.

THE NEXT DAY, MY CELLMATE INTRODUCED ME TO HIS FRIENDS. ALL OF THEM WERE INVOLVED IN THE PIETY STREET SHOOTOUT. THESE GUYS DEFENDED THE RIGHTS OF THEIR BROTHERS, GUNS IN HAND, STARING DOWN THE COPS' BARRELS.

THEY WERE DRIVEN BY A HIGHER POLITICAL AWARENESS, ONE THAT I LACKED. MEETING THEM SPARKED MY EDUCATION, AND I GREW TO BE MORE THAN A PETTY THIEF.

I MET CHARLES SCOTT

ALTON EDWARDS

DONALD GUYTON*

RONALD AILSWORTH

*SINCE CONVERTING TO ISLAM, HE GOES BY THE NAME MALIK RAHIM. DURING THE 2000S, RAHIM WOULD BE A VOCAL SUPPORTER FOR THE LIBERATION OF THE ANGOLA 3.

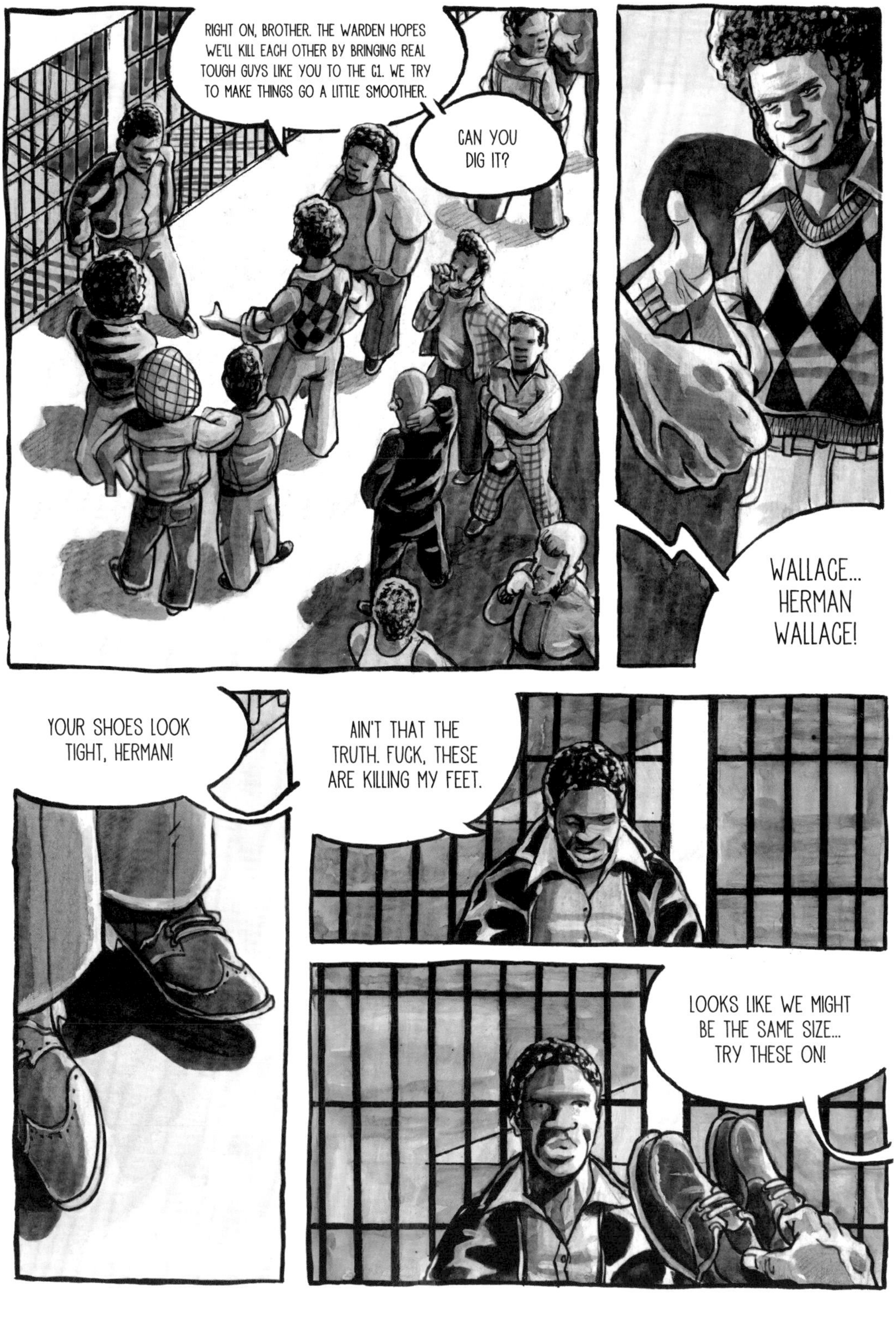
RIGHT ON, BROTHER. THE WARDEN HOPES WE'LL KILL EACH OTHER BY BRINGING REAL TOUGH GUYS LIKE YOU TO THE C1. WE TRY TO MAKE THINGS GO A LITTLE SMOOTHER.
CAN YOU DIG IT?
WALLACE... HERMAN WALLACE!
YOUR SHOES LOOK TIGHT, HERMAN!
AIN'T THAT THE TRUTH. FUCK, THESE ARE KILLING MY FEET.
LOOKS LIKE WE MIGHT BE THE SAME SIZE... TRY THESE ON!

THEN HE LEFT WITHOUT A WORD. I UNDERSTOOD THEN WHAT IT WOULD MEAN TO BE A PART OF THE GROUP, AND THE BEHAVIOR I WOULD HAVE TO MIRROR IN ORDER TO BECOME THEIR BROTHER.

SOON AFTER, AND ON SEVERAL OCCASIONS, WE FOUND OURSELVES TOGETHER, FACING THE TRIALS FOR OUR RESPECTIVE CRIMES,

WHICH IS HOW I MET THE WOMEN IN OUR GROUP.

LIKE CATHERINE BOURNES

LEAH HODGES,

AND ELAINE E-BABY.

THROUGH THESE BRIEF AND FURTIVE ENCOUNTERS, WE BUILT A STRONG FAMILY BOND.

IN THE C1, THE PRISON'S GOALS WERE CLEAR. MOST OF THE INMATES WERE ALIGNED WITH THE BLACK PANTHERS.

ALBERT WOODFOX REJOINED US IN THE FALL OF 1970.

A NEW ONE?

YEAH, ALL I KNOW IS THAT HE'S COMING FROM THE TOMBS!

THE TOMBS IN NEW YORK?

YEAH, NEW YORK, ALRIGHT. I'VE HEARD IT'S EVEN WORSE THAN HERE. THEY FUCKING RIOTED OVER THERE. MAN, IF HE WAS A PART OF ALL THAT, WE NEED TO SHOW HIM SOME RESPECT.

OH COME ON, WOODFOX, CHEER UP... YOU'RE BACK HOME!

ALBERT AND I WERE TRANSFERRED TO ANGOLA IN 1971.

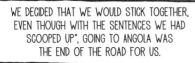

ANGOLA
20 MILES

WE DECIDED THAT WE WOULD STICK TOGETHER, EVEN THOUGH WITH THE SENTENCES WE HAD SCOOPED UP*, GOING TO ANGOLA WAS THE END OF THE ROAD FOR US.

DURING OUR YEAR TOGETHER AT THE C1, ALBERT AND I HAD FORMED A TIGHT BOND. I WAS IMPRESSED BY WHAT HE'D BEEN THROUGH. HE'D SEEN SOME SHIT!

ANOTHER CHANGE OF ADDRESS...IF I COUNTED BACK TO THE BEGINNING, YOU COULD FILL A BOOK.

*50 YEARS FOR WOODFOX AND 200 FOR WALLACE, ACCORDING TO MALIK RAHIM.

40

ALBERT WOODFOX

I GOT TWO YEARS AND THEY SENT ME TO THIBODAUX TO DO MY TIME. I DIDN'T THINK MUCH BACK THEN. I ESCAPED SUDDENLY, ON A WHIM.

FUCK, 2 YEARS MIGHT AS WELL BE 2 CENTURIES. AND IN THIS HICK TOWN IN THE MIDDLE OF NOWHERE WHERE I DON'T KNOW ANYONE. BUNCH OF ASSHOLES.

I DON'T HAVE A CHOICE. MOM NEEDS ME, I CAN'T LEAVE HER LIKE THAT.

I HID OUT NEAR A CONSTRUCTION SITE FOR A DAY, AND WHEN NIGHT CAME, I CLIMBED INTO A CEMENT TRUCK TO SLEEP. THE KEYS WERE IN THE IGNITION. I HIT THE GAS.

NEW ORLEANS, I'M HERE. I'M COMING HOME, BABY!

THE FREEWAY WAS NOT A PROBLEM, BUT ONCE I GOT INTO THE CITY

HMM.... HMM.... INTERESTING.

I STOPPED AT A LIGHT. COPS WERE IDLING NEXT TO ME AND STARTED TO LOOK AT ME FUNNY.

AND WHAT DO YOU HAVE TO SAY IN YOUR DEFENSE?

A BLACK KID AT THE WHEEL OF THIS HUGE TRUCK, IT DIDN'T LOOK RIGHT. I JUMPED OUT AND STARTED TO RUN.

I WAS HOMESICK, YOUR HONOR.

THE COPS SHOT AT ME. I KEPT RUNNING. THEY DIDN'T GET ME TILL THE NEXT MORNING.

WITH MY PREVIOUS CONVICTIONS AND THE ESCAPE BEING TWICE AS BAD, I GOT 50 YEARS.

THIS TIME, I HAD A GOOD REASON TO GET OUT OF THERE.

IT WAS TIME FOR ME TO GET SOME FRESH AIR. I MADE IT ALL THE WAY TO NEW YORK, WHERE I GOT TO HARLEM. IT WAS REALLY HAPPENING THERE, IT WAS NOTHING LIKE I'D SEEN IN NEW ORLEANS.

THE PANTHERS WERE ORGANIZING EVERYWHERE. I HAD NEVER SEEN BROTHERS SO PROUD.

HEY, MY BROTHER! WHAT ARE YOU WAITING FOR?

I'M NOT GONNA DO ALL THE WORK!

COME ON, TAKE THESE AND SHARE 'EM.

JEAN GENET speaks to the students

FRENCH AUTHOR AND PLAYWRIGHT SPEAKS ABOUT BOBBY SEALE AND THE BLACK PANTHER PARTY AND THE CONDITIONS OF BLACK PEOPLE IN AMERICA.

SPONSORED BY NYU STUDENT LAWYER'S GUILD

Monday
at 2:00p.m
grand ballroom
student union bldg.
NYU

donations welcome

DESPITE MY LACK OF POLITICAL AWARENESS, I UNDERSTOOD THAT THIS WAS THE TRUE VOICE OF SOCIAL JUSTICE FOR ALL.

MY BROTHERS!
MY SISTERS!

YOU WANT FREEDOM! YOU WANT JUSTICE! THE END OF POLICE BRUTALITY, THE END OF THE POLICE INVASION OF OUR COMMUNITIES! WE MUST ORGANIZE OURSELVES AND DEVELOP A POLICY OF SHARING WITH EACH OTHER. WE MUST BREAK DOWN THE WALLS BETWEEN THOSE WHO HAVE EVERYTHING AND THOSE WITH NOTHING! THE BLACK NATION WILL NEVER BE A UTOPIA UNLESS WE BUILD IT TOGETHER!

MY BROTHERS, MY SISTERS, AND ALL OPPRESSED PEOPLE FORCED INTO RACIAL OR SOCIAL SUBMISSION! WE MUST DO EVERYTHING NECESSARY TO DESTROY THE MYTH THAT THE UNITES STATES OF AMERICA IS A DEMOCRACY!

YOU GOT ID, KID?

THE TOMBS, MANHATTAN.

THIS WAS MY FIRST AND LAST RETURN TO COUNTY JAIL.

THIS IS WHERE I WOULD SOLIDIFY MY POLITICAL BELIEFS, WITH MY NEW BROTHERS IN ARMS, ALL IN PRISON TOGETHER. WE FORMED A COALITION OF INMATES WHO WERE READY TO DENOUNCE THE INHUMANE CONDITIONS AT THE PRISON. THE GUARDS HAD NO IDEA.

WE ROSE UP AND REVOLTED.

46

THE POLICE WERE IN THE STREETS BELOW, TRYING TO EXTERMINATE US LIKE RATS WITH TEARGAS GRENADES. SO WE THREW DEAD RATS BACK AT THEM, THE PRISON WAS FULL OF THEM. AFTER THE RIOT, THEY DECIDED TO RETURN ME TO LOUISIANA, SO THAT I COULD DO THE REST OF MY TIME AT ANGOLA.

WELCOME TO ANGOLA. YOU WILL SOON JOIN THE GENERAL POPULATION. MOST OF YOU WILL WORK IN THE SUGARCANE FIELDS. YOU WILL WORK EVERY DAY, EXCEPT FOR SATURDAYS AND SUNDAYS. DURING HARVEST SEASON, MANY OF YOU WILL CONTINUE TO WORK. REFUSAL TO WORK WILL NOT BE TOLERATED.

POLITICAL STATEMENTS WILL NOT BE TOLERATED.

YOU ARE HERE TO DO YOUR TIME, AND YOU WILL DO IT, EVEN IF THAT MEANS WE HAVE TO KILL YOU AND BURY YOU HERE AT POINT LOOKOUT. DO YOU UNDERSTAND?

HMM. I THINK I'M HEADED FOR THE FIELDS, THEY KNOW I CAN WIELD A MACHETE*. I HOPE YOU HAVE BETTER LUCK.

*WALLACE HAD PREVIOUSLY SPENT SEVERAL MONTHS AT ANGOLA.

48

WE WERE BOTH ORDERED TO WORK IN THE CANE FIELDS.

THOSE WHO COULDN'T KEEP UP THE PACE WERE PENALIZED WITH DISCIPLINARY REPORTS.

THESE REPORTS ALLOWED THE ADMINISTRATION TO FORCE INMATES TO WORK ON WEEKENDS AND HOLIDAYS.

SO WE DECIDED TO WORK MORE SLOWLY

AND TO HELP THOSE THAT COULDN'T ALWAYS KEEP UP.

TO CONQUER THE AMERICAN SLAVE SYSTEM THAT RULED ANGOLA WE KNEW THAT WE NEEDED TO ORGANIZE AND TO ACT. HERMAN AND I DECIDED TO FOUND THE FIRST EVER CHAPTER OF THE BLACK PANTHERS INSIDE A PRISON. THE PARTY'S CENTRAL COMMITTEE GAVE US PERMISSION.

WE NEEDED A PROGRAM TO MAKE SURE THAT THIS WOULD BE MORE THAN JUST TALK.

THE PROGRAM CONSISTED OF POLITICAL MEETINGS TO MAKE BLACK AND WHITE PRISONERS AWARE OF THEIR PRESENT CONDITION,

PHYSICAL TRAINING, LESSONS IN PHYSICAL DEFENSE, HELPING THOSE THAT WEREN'T ABLE, AND TEACHING THE LESS EDUCATED TO READ.

THANKS TO OUR ACTIONS, WE HAD RECLAIMED THE PRISON FROM THOSE INMATES THAT HAD BENEFITED FROM THE EXPLOITATION OF OTHERS.

WE HAD ALMOST SUCCEEDED IN ERADICATING RAPE AND SEX SLAVERY.

ONE MORNING IN APRIL 1972 WOULD TURN OUR LIVES UPSIDE DOWN.

YOU SURE ARE SEXY, AGENT MILLER, BUT IT'S ALREADY 6 AM.

I'LL WAIT FOR YOU IN THE CAR, BABY!

SEE YOU AT WORK, BRENT!

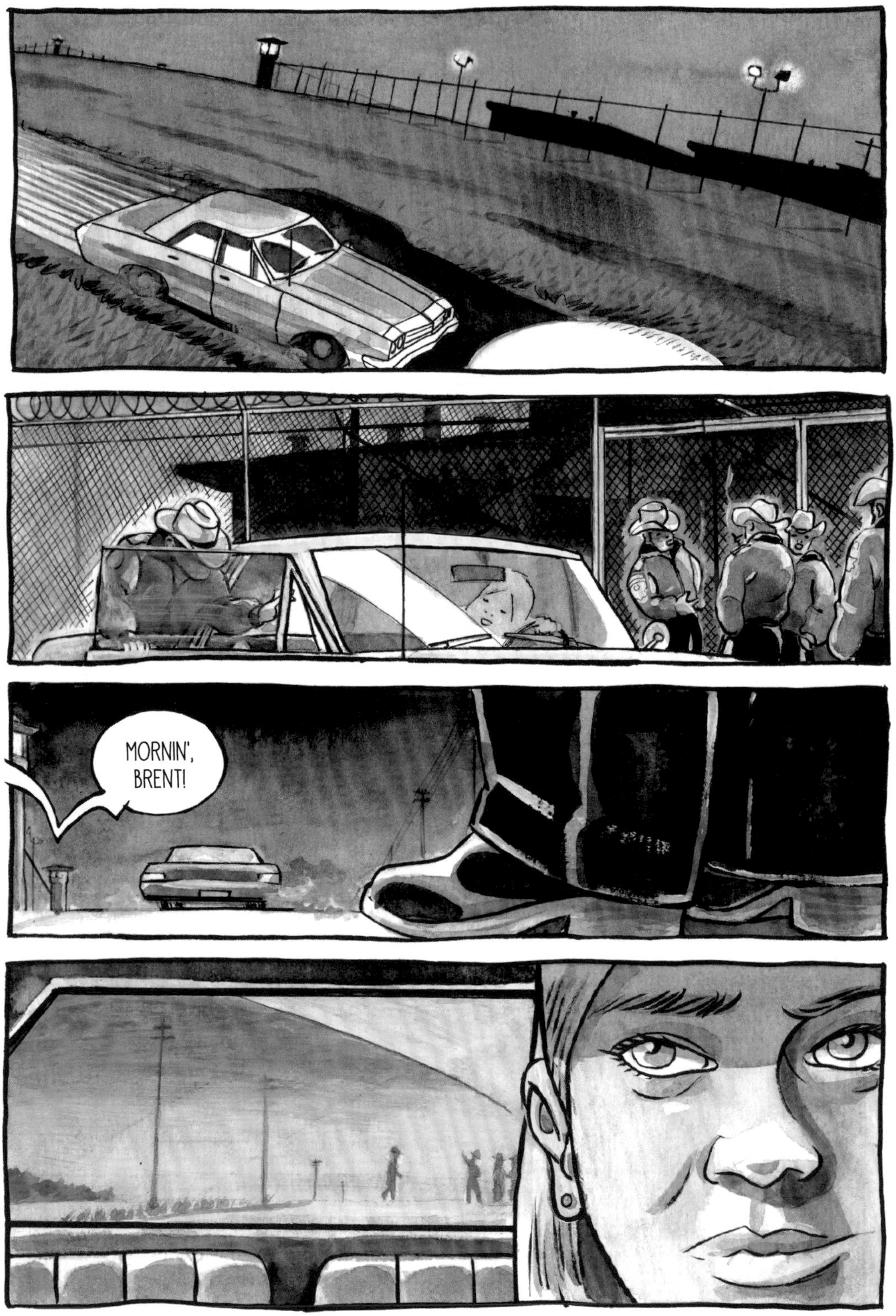
MORNIN', BRENT!

THERE WAS A PROTEST IN THE CAFETERIA THAT MORNING.

OK, I'LL CALL THE WARDEN.

WHAT?! A STRIKE?! HOW MANY GUARDS ARE THERE? HM, HM, GOOD. GET ALL THE GUYS YOU NEED AND SHUT THAT DOWN!

WARDEN

BLING

HEARD! YES, SIR!

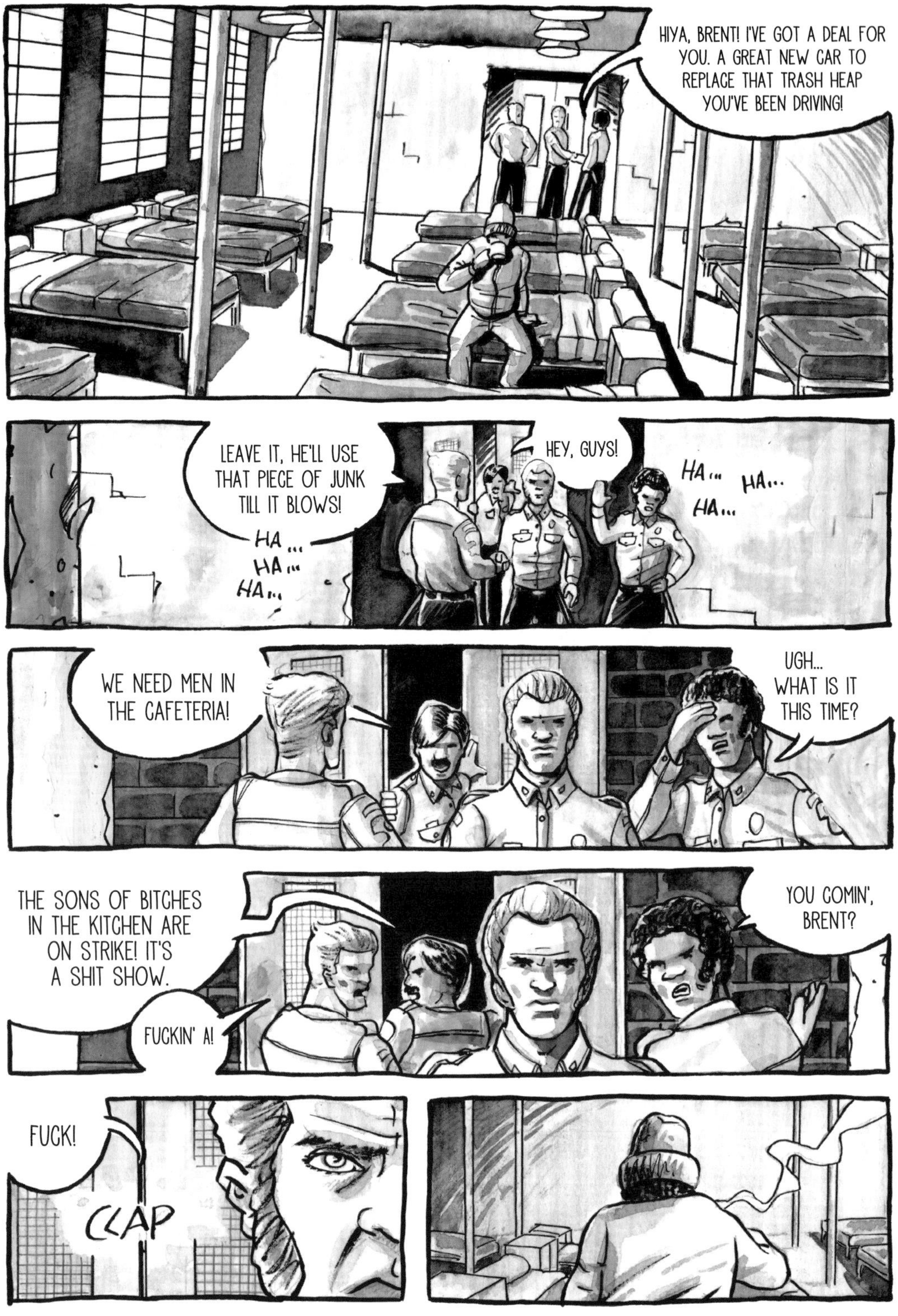
HIYA, BRENT! I'VE GOT A DEAL FOR YOU. A GREAT NEW CAR TO REPLACE THAT TRASH HEAP YOU'VE BEEN DRIVING!
LEAVE IT, HE'LL USE THAT PIECE OF JUNK TILL IT BLOWS!
HA... HA... HA...
HEY, GUYS!
HA... HA... HA...
WE NEED MEN IN THE CAFETERIA!
UGH... WHAT IS IT THIS TIME?
THE SONS OF BITCHES IN THE KITCHEN ARE ON STRIKE! IT'S A SHIT SHOW.
YOU COMIN', BRENT?
FUCKIN' A!
FUCK!
CLAP

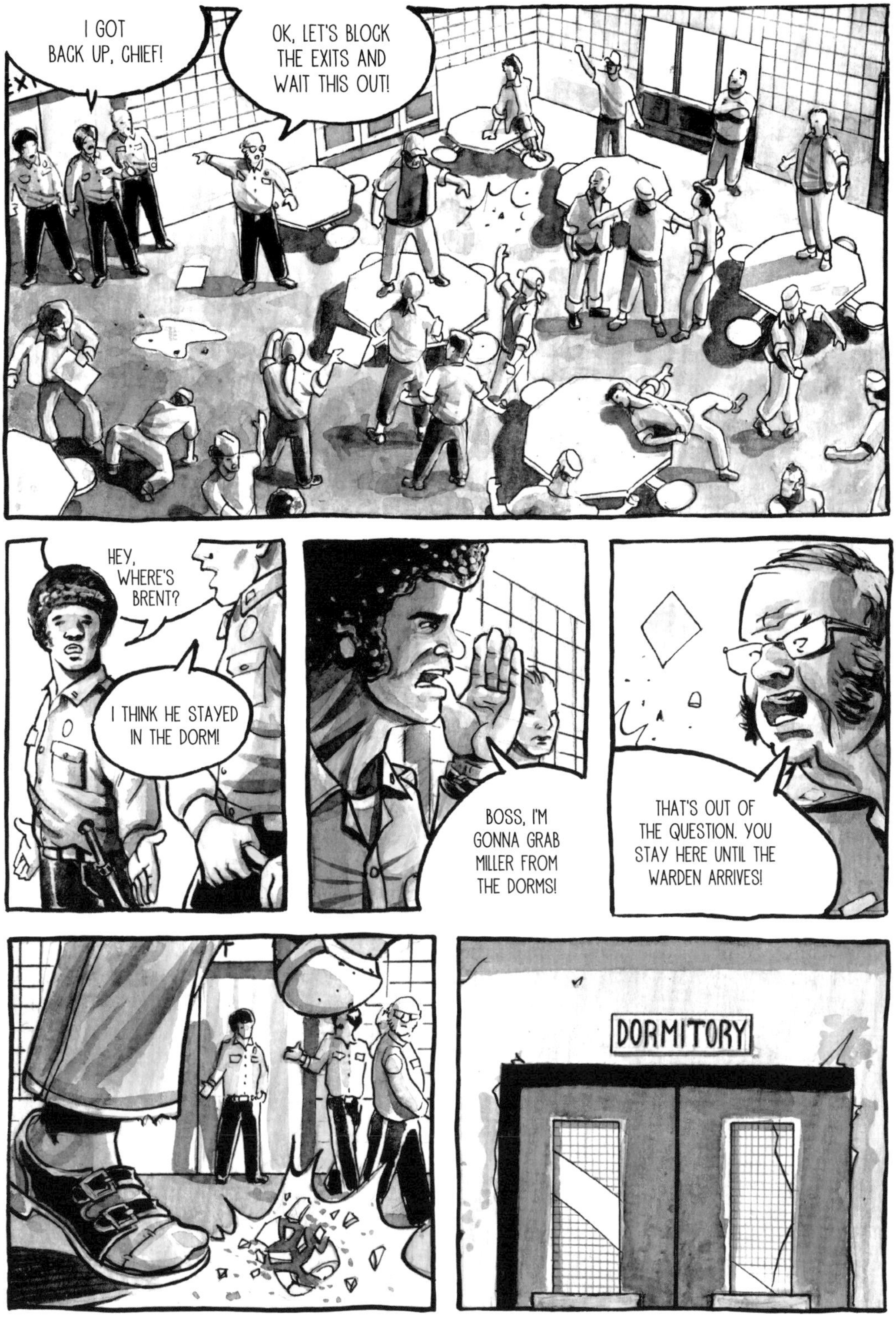
I GOT BACK UP, CHIEF!
OK, LET'S BLOCK THE EXITS AND WAIT THIS OUT!
HEY, WHERE'S BRENT?
I THINK HE STAYED IN THE DORM!
BOSS, I'M GONNA GRAB MILLER FROM THE DORMS!
THAT'S OUT OF THE QUESTION. YOU STAY HERE UNTIL THE WARDEN ARRIVES!
DORMITORY

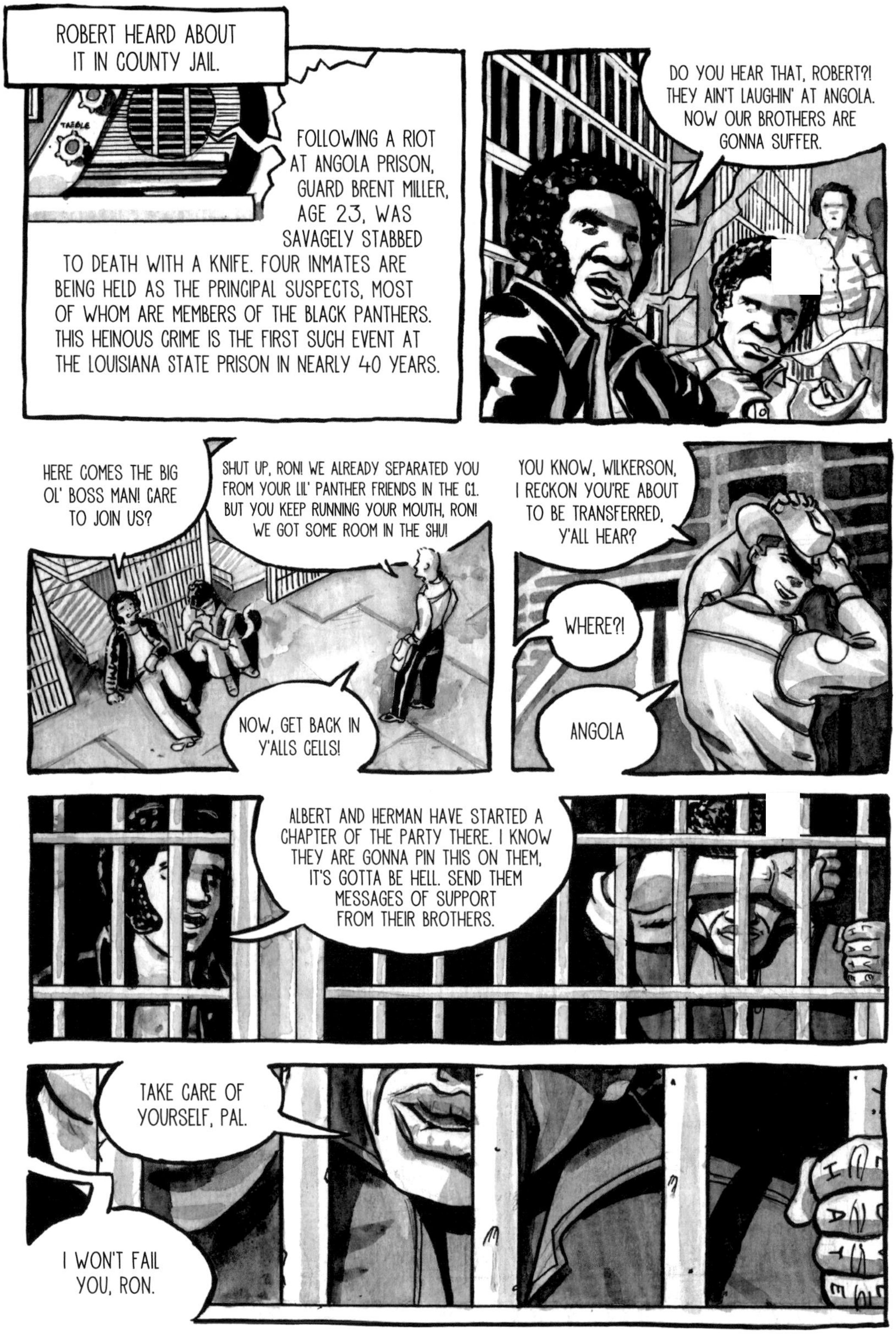
ROBERT HEARD ABOUT IT IN COUNTY JAIL.
FOLLOWING A RIOT AT ANGOLA PRISON, GUARD BRENT MILLER, AGE 23, WAS SAVAGELY STABBED TO DEATH WITH A KNIFE. FOUR INMATES ARE BEING HELD AS THE PRINCIPAL SUSPECTS, MOST OF WHOM ARE MEMBERS OF THE BLACK PANTHERS. THIS HEINOUS CRIME IS THE FIRST SUCH EVENT AT THE LOUISIANA STATE PRISON IN NEARLY 40 YEARS.
DO YOU HEAR THAT, ROBERT?! THEY AIN'T LAUGHIN' AT ANGOLA. NOW OUR BROTHERS ARE GONNA SUFFER.
HERE COMES THE BIG OL' BOSS MAN! CARE TO JOIN US?
SHUT UP, RON! WE ALREADY SEPARATED YOU FROM YOUR LIL' PANTHER FRIENDS IN THE C1. BUT YOU KEEP RUNNING YOUR MOUTH, RON! WE GOT SOME ROOM IN THE SHU!
NOW, GET BACK IN Y'ALLS CELLS!
YOU KNOW, WILKERSON, I RECKON YOU'RE ABOUT TO BE TRANSFERRED, Y'ALL HEAR?
WHERE?!
ANGOLA
ALBERT AND HERMAN HAVE STARTED A CHAPTER OF THE PARTY THERE. I KNOW THEY ARE GONNA PIN THIS ON THEM, IT'S GOTTA BE HELL. SEND THEM MESSAGES OF SUPPORT FROM THEIR BROTHERS.
TAKE CARE OF YOURSELF, PAL.
I WON'T FAIL YOU, RON.

HAVE COURAGE MY CHILD, YOUR HUSBAND IS WITH THE GOOD LORD NOW.

PLEASE TAKE ME HOME.

SURE THING, FATHER. LET'S GO.

POOR THING, IT'S AWFUL. JUST MARRIED AND ALREADY A WIDOW!

HAVE YOU FOUND THE MURDERER?

OH YES, REVEREND. WE EVEN CAUGHT FOUR! TWO OF 'EM ARE THOSE BLACK PANTHER BASTARDS, WALLACE AND WOODFOX. THEY'VE BEEN CAUSING A RUCKUS SINCE THEY ARRIVED. THEY THINK THEY CAN RUN THE PRISON. WE GOT 'EM ON OUR RADAR NOW, AND WE DON'T SLIP UP.

BLACK PANTHERS. THESE MARXIST VERMIN CLAWED THEIR WAY INTO OUR PRISONS. THESE COMMIES MUST BE PUT IN THEIR PLACE.

ROBERT KING

EARLY MAY 1972, IT WAS MY TURN TO BE TRANSFERRED TO ANGOLA.

AFTER THE YOUNG GUARD'S KILLING, THE PRISON WAS ON TOTAL LOCKDOWN. VISITS WERE SUSPENDED, WHICH ALLOWED THE GUARDS TO ABUSE US WITH IMPUNITY. THE SEARCH FOR BRENT MILLER'S MURDERER LED TO A WITCH-HUNT THAT I COULDN'T ESCAPE, DESPITE THE FACT THAT I HAD NOT YET ARRIVED AT ANGOLA WHEN HE WAS KILLED.

I WAS IMMEDIATELY PLACED IN AN ISOLATION UNIT. THERE I WITNESSED THE VIOLENT HUMILIATIONS THAT THE SUSPECTS WERE SUBJECTED TO. THEY WERE THROWN NAKED, THEIR SKULLS CRACKED, INTO COMPLETELY EMPTY CELLS, WHERE THEY WERE BEATEN REGULARLY WITH BASEBALL BATS AND GOLF CLUBS.

NOT A SINGLE WHITE PRISONER WAS SUBJECTED TO THIS TYPE OF TREATMENT. NONE OF THEM WERE BEATEN OR THROWN INTO THE HOLE, OR EVEN ASKED ABOUT THE GUARD'S MURDER.

58

AFTER SEVERAL DAYS, I APPEARED BEFORE A DISCIPLINARY HEARING AND WAS FOUND GUILTY OF WANTING TO PLAY THE ROLE OF A LAWYER FOR THE OTHER INMATES. I WAS BEING PUNISHED FOR MY POLITICAL ACTIVITY WITH THE BLACK PANTHERS.

THEY SENT ME TO THE NOTORIOUS RED HAT CELL BLOCK,

...WHERE THE CELLS WERE NOTHING MORE THAN A CONCRETE BENCH, A TOILET BOWL AND SINK THAT WERE USUALLY OUT OF ORDER, AND WHERE WE WERE BARELY FED.

AT THE END OF MAY, I APPEARED AGAIN, THIS TIME BEFORE A COMMISSION FOR THE CLASSIFICATION OF INMATES, LED BY SEVERAL OF THE PRISON'S GUARDS. I RECOGNIZED HILTON BUTLER, THE WARDEN'S RIGHT HAND MAN, WHO STOOD AND WALKED TOWARDS THE EXIT, LOOKING AT ME WITH DISGUST.

Y'ALL KNOW WHERE I STAND.

I HAD NOTHING TO SAY. THE COMMITTEE DECIDED IMMEDIATELY THAT I PROBABLY HAD SOMETHING TO DO WITH THE MURDER OF BRENT MILLER AND THAT I WOULD BE SUBJECTED TO FURTHER QUESTIONING. I WAS THEREFORE SENT TO LIVE IN ISOLATION, WHICH I WOULD NOT LEAVE FOR THE NEXT 29 YEARS.

I HAD NEVER MET BRENT MILLER. WE NEVER HAD A CHANCE TO CROSS PATHS AT ANGOLA...

BECAUSE HE HAD DIED BEFORE I ARRIVED! IT WAS EASY TO CHECK.

*RED HAT OPENED IN 1932 AND CLOSED FORTY YEARS LATER. IT WAS KNOWN AS THE WORST PART OF ANGOLA, AND NAMED FOR THE CAPS WORN BY THE SLAVES THAT HAD PREVIOUSLY TOILED IN THE FIELDS.

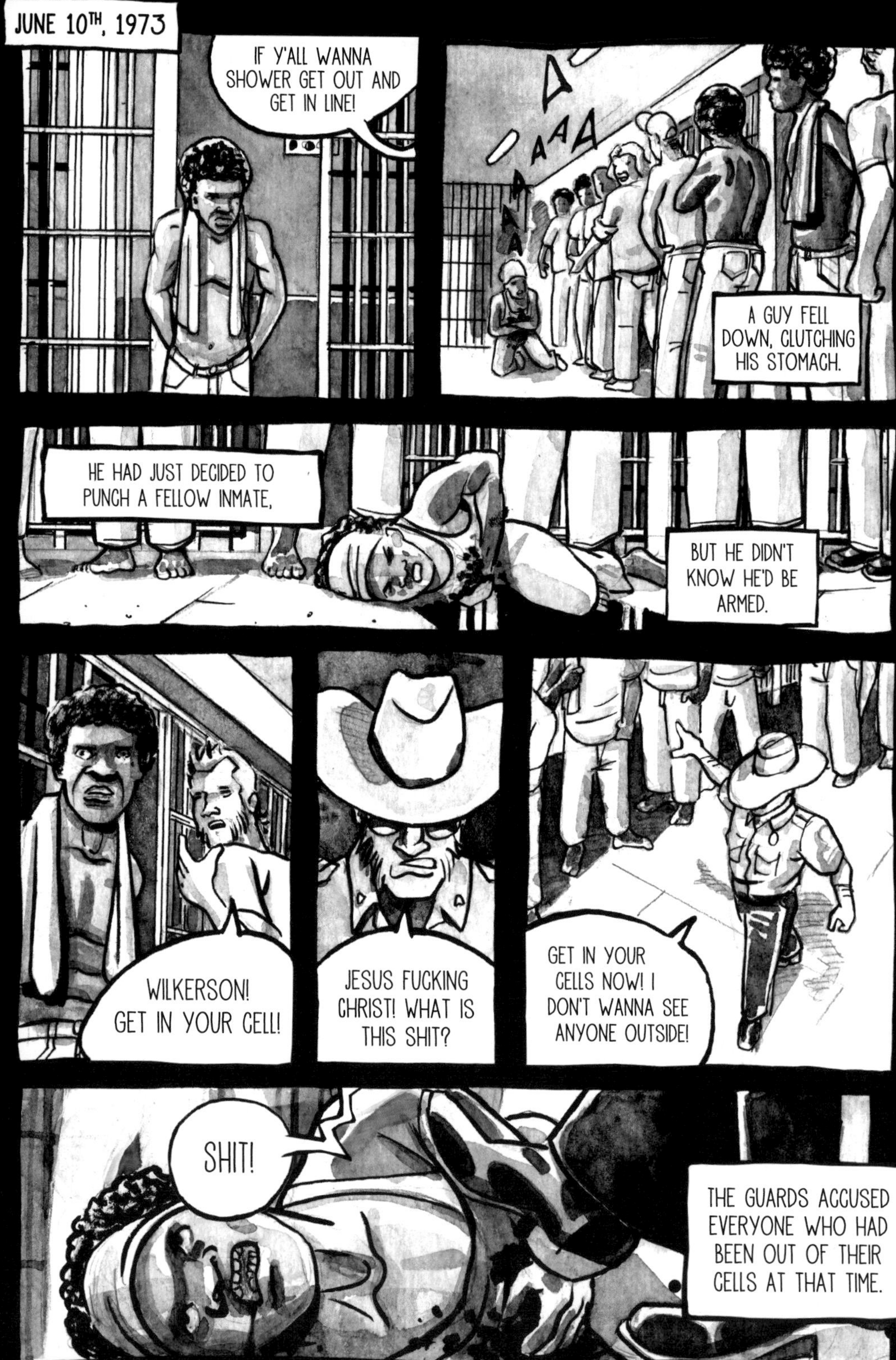
JUNE 10TH, 1973
IF Y'ALL WANNA SHOWER GET OUT AND GET IN LINE!
AAAAA
A GUY FELL DOWN, CLUTCHING HIS STOMACH.
HE HAD JUST DECIDED TO PUNCH A FELLOW INMATE,
BUT HE DIDN'T KNOW HE'D BE ARMED.
WILKERSON! GET IN YOUR CELL!
JESUS FUCKING CHRIST! WHAT IS THIS SHIT?
GET IN YOUR CELLS NOW! I DON'T WANNA SEE ANYONE OUTSIDE!
SHIT!
THE GUARDS ACCUSED EVERYONE WHO HAD BEEN OUT OF THEIR CELLS AT THAT TIME.

A LITTLE WHILE LATER, NINE INMATES WERE CLEARED. ONLY GRADY BREWER AND I WERE LEFT, SO WE WERE ACCUSED OF KILLING AUGUST KELLY.

WILKERSON! HANDS ON YOUR HEAD! DON'T MOVE!

OCTOBER 10TH, 1973

YOU AIN'T GOT NOTHING TO WORRY ABOUT, WILKERSON! I KILLED THAT FOOL! THAT LITTLE SHIT CAME AT ME, WANTED MY SKIN, IT WAS SELF-DEFENSE!

WE WERE BOTH SENT TO A COURT IN ST. FRANCISVILLE.

THE GUARD ON DUTY THE MORNING OF JUNE 10TH, 1973 DID NOT SEE ME PARTICIPATE IN THE MURDER.

THE LAWYER'S SPEECH EXPLAINED THAT BLOOD HAD BEEN FOUND ON ONLY ONE OF THE NINE KNIVES SEIZED FROM THE INMATES SURROUNDING THE BODY.* MY FINGERPRINTS WERE NOWHERE TO BE FOUND AND THERE WASN'T ANY BLOOD ON MY CLOTHES.

GRADY BREWER'S SHIRT WAS COVERED IN BLOOD, AND HE DID NOT ONCE CLAIM TO BE INNOCENT.

I KILLED HIM TO SAVE MY OWN SKIN!

SHUT UP!

YOUR HONOR, WE HAVE NOT BEEN GIVEN TIME TO SPEAK WITH A LAWYER.

SHUT UP!

BECAUSE WE WANTED TO SPEAK, WE WERE FORCED TO SIT THROUGH THE REST OF OUR TRIAL WITH OUR MOUTHS TAPED AND OUR HANDS CUFFED. WE WERE SENTENCED TO LIFE. I FILED AN APPEAL AND MY SENTENCING WAS POSTPONED. THE STATE ORDERED A NEW TRIAL TO TAKE PLACE, NOT DUE TO THE WEAKNESS OF THEIR EVIDENCE BUT INSTEAD THE JUDGE'S ABUSE OF POWER AND THE FACT THAT WE HAD BEEN RESTRAINED AND STIFLED.

IN 1975, AFTER THE SECOND TRIAL WAS HELD, I WAS ONCE AGAIN SENTENCED TO LIFE.

*IT WAS NOT WISE TO LIVE IN ANGOLA WITHOUT SOME KIND OF MAKESHIFT WEAPON.

IN JANUARY 1974, THOUGH ALBERT WOODFOX HAD BEEN SENTENCED TO LIFE THE YEAR BEFORE,

WALLACE, JACKSON, AND MONTAGUE APPEARED TOGETHER AND STOOD TRIAL FOR THE MURDER OF BRENT MILLER BEFORE THE COURT OF ST. FRANCISVILLE.

CHESTER JACKSON, GUILTY!

JACKSON CLAIMED THAT HE HELD BRENT MILLER FROM BEHIND SO THAT WOODFOX AND WALLACE COULD STAB HIM.

GILBERT MONTAGUE, NOT GUILTY!

JACKSON WAS NO LONGER SURE AS TO WHETHER HE HAD SEEN MONTAGUE PARTICIPATE IN THE MURDER, SO THE CHARGES WERE DROPPED.

HERMAN WALLACE, GUILTY!

MAY I ASK A QUESTION?

GO ON, I'M LISTENING.

WHERE ARE THE BLACK PEOPLE ON THIS JURY?!

GET HIM OUT OF HERE!

THIS TRIAL WILL END IN CALM AND ORDER!

NO!

HOW CAN YOU SAY THAT MY BROTHER KILLED THIS MAN? HE IS NOT A MURDERER, HE HAS NEVER KILLED ANYONE!

VIKKI?!

BE QUIET!

NO MOTHER, I WILL NOT BE QUIET!

DEAR LORD...

TAKE CARE OF YOURSELF, VIKKI!

LOWER THOSE FINGERS, WALLACE!

MY FRIENDS ALBERT WOODFOX AND HERMAN WALLACE BOTH FOUND THEMSELVES SENTENCED TO LIFE AND ALL THREE OF US WERE DEEMED DANGEROUS TO THE PRISON'S ORDER AND SECURITY BY THE ADMINISTRATION. WE WERE HELD IN ISOLATION. AT ANGOLA, THIS MEANT THAT WE COULDN'T WORK. WE DIDN'T HAVE PERMISSION TO GO ANYWHERE OR TO PARTICIPATE IN ANY ACTIVITIES. IN SHORT, WE LOST ALL FORMS OF SOCIAL ENGAGEMENT.

THE THREE OF US ACCUMULATED HUNDREDS OF HEARINGS BEFORE THE COMMITTEE TO REVISIT OUR STATUS AND EACH TIME WE HEARD THE SAME DECISION: MUST REMAIN IN CCR DUE TO THE NATURE OF THE ORIGINAL REASON FOR LOCKDOWN. DESPITE THE ADMINISTRATION'S RELENTLESS DETERMINATION TO KEEP US IN ISOLATION,

ONE OF OUR FIRST BATTLES WAS ABOUT MEALTIMES. THE TRAYS WERE DROPPED ON THE GRIMY FLOORS AND WE EITHER HAD TO EAT BETWEEN THE BARS OR TRY AND SLIDE THE TRAY UNDER THE CELL DOOR. WE CONVINCED THE OTHER INMATES TO JOIN US IN A HUNGER STRIKE THAT LASTED 45 DAYS.

THE PRISON ADMINISTRATION ULTIMATELY GAVE IN AND WE GOT AN OPENING FOR THE TRAYS IN THE CELL'S BARS. BUT IT WOULD TAKE 18 MONTHS UNTIL THEY WERE INSTALLED.

LATER, IN 1977, WE WERE FACED WITH AN EVEN MORE REVOLTING PRACTICE THAT HAD ALWAYS TAKEN PLACE IN THE PRISON: ANAL CAVITY SEARCHES.

GIVEN THE FACT THAT WE WERE HANDCUFFED AND IN CHAINS EVERY TIME WE LEFT THE CELL THESE SEARCHES WERE COMPLETELY USELESS. IT WAS A TRADITION DATING BACK TO THE SLAVE TRADE THAT THE GUARDS WANTED TO KEEP ALIVE, AS SLAVES HAD ALWAYS BEEN STRIP SEARCHED AND EXAMINED PRIOR TO THEIR SALE.

AFTER MONTHS OF FUTILE NEGOTIATIONS WITH THE GUARDS, WE DECIDED THAT WE WOULD NO LONGER ALLOW THEM TO DO IT. WE WOULD NO LONGER TAKE PART IN OUR OWN DEBASEMENT. WE KNEW THAT THIS WOULD HAVE CONSEQUENCES, BUT WE WERE READY TO SACRIFICE EVERYTHING, AND EVEN PREPARED TO DIE.

WE WERE TO BE SEPARATED, SPLIT UP, ISOLATED. AWARE OF THE DANGERS AHEAD, WE DECIDED TO EXCHANGE CONTACT INFORMATION FOR OUR LOVED ONES WITH EACH OTHER. SOONER OR LATER, EACH ONE OF US WOULD HAVE TO GO THROUGH WITH IT. WHEN MY TURN CAME, I WAS CHAINED AND TAKEN TO A DISTANT OFFICE WHERE THE GUARDS AWAITED ME, ALL STANDING AGAINST THE WALL.

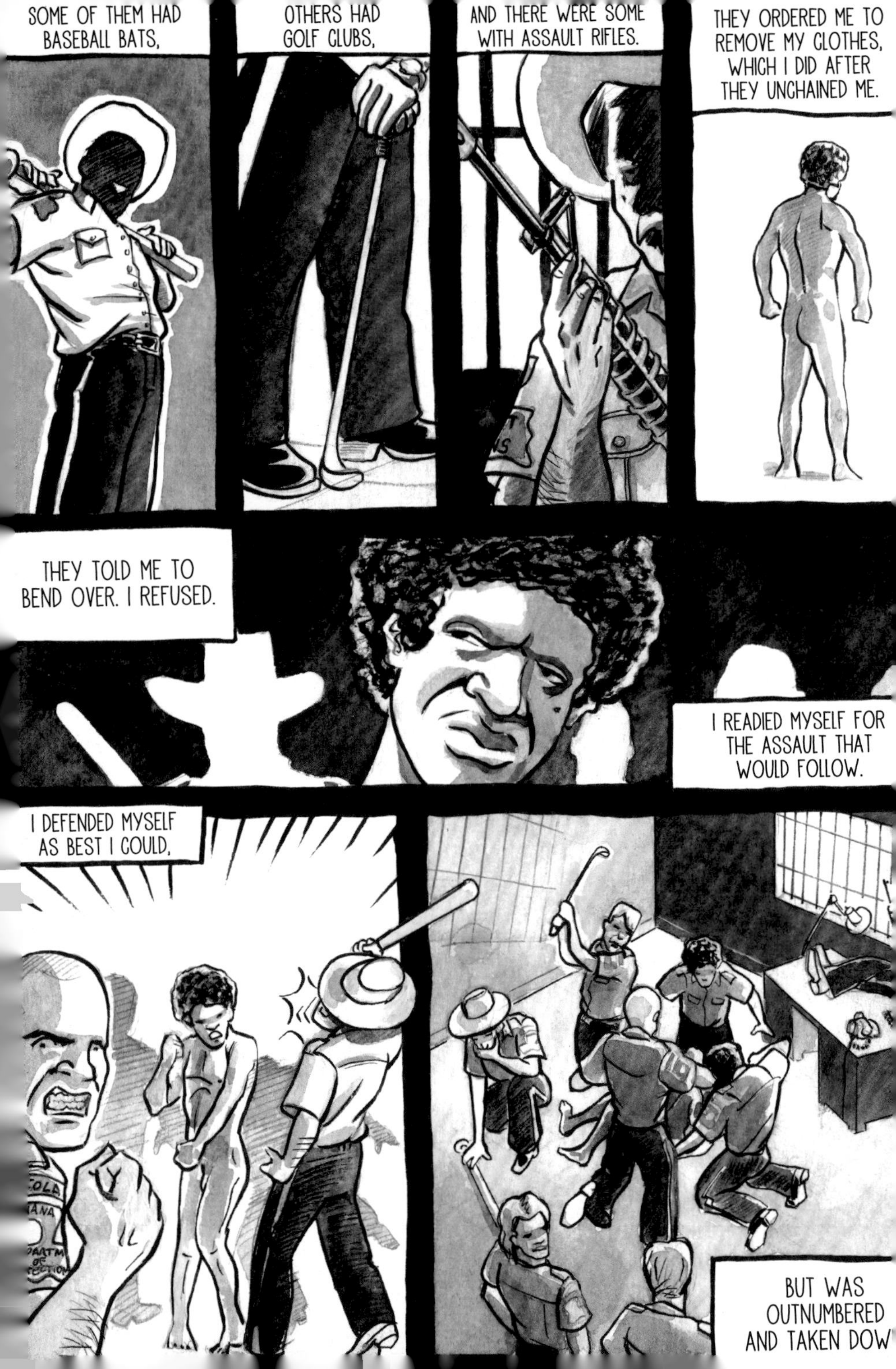
SOME OF THEM HAD BASEBALL BATS,
OTHERS HAD GOLF CLUBS,
AND THERE WERE SOME WITH ASSAULT RIFLES.
THEY ORDERED ME TO REMOVE MY CLOTHES, WHICH I DID AFTER THEY UNCHAINED ME.
THEY TOLD ME TO BEND OVER. I REFUSED.
I READIED MYSELF FOR THE ASSAULT THAT WOULD FOLLOW.
I DEFENDED MYSELF AS BEST I COULD,
BUT WAS OUTNUMBERED AND TAKEN DOW

I WAS TRANSPORTED TO THE HOSPITAL, WHERE MY WOUNDS WERE EXAMINED, THEN IMMEDIATELY SENT TO CAMP J, THE NEWLY BUILT DISCIPLINARY FACILITY. I WAS ACCUSED OF ATTACKING THE GUARDS, BUT THOSE CHARGES WERE LATER DROPPED.

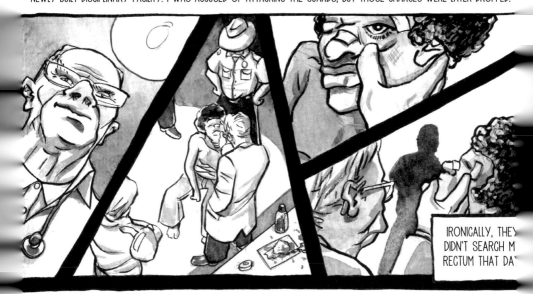

IRONICALLY, THEY DIDN'T SEARCH MY RECTUM THAT DAY.

DURING THIS TIME, WOODFOX WAS STILL IN CCR, BUT HE WAS ABLE TO GET IN TOUCH WITH MY PEOPLE ON THE OUTSIDE. THEY CALLED THE PRISON TO INQUIRE ABOUT MY HEALTH.

THIS SPARED ME FROM MORE BRUTALITY, AND MAYBE EVEN SAVED MY LIFE: SOMEONE ON THE OUTSIDE WAS WORRIED ABOUT ME.

OUR ACTIONS YIELDED RESULTS, AND IN 1978 THE PRACTICE WAS BANNED.

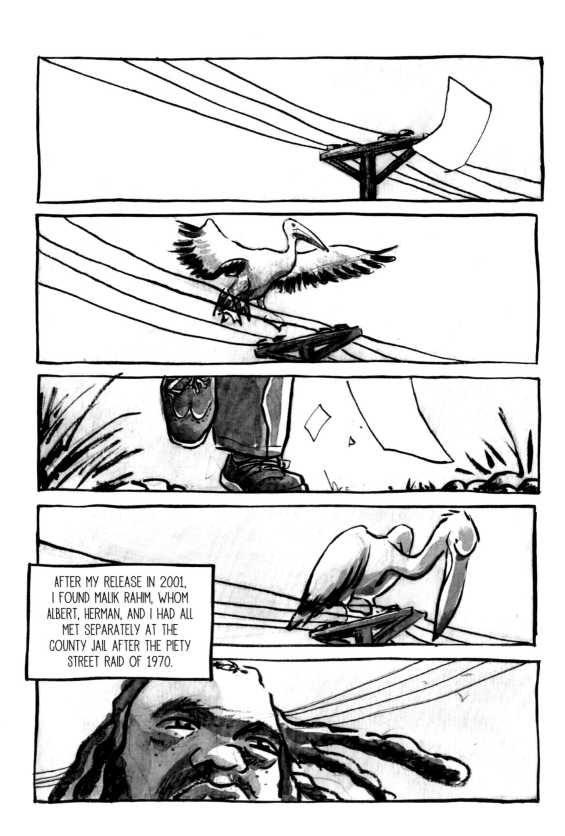

AFTER MY RELEASE IN 2001, I FOUND MALIK RAHIM, WHOM ALBERT, HERMAN, AND I HAD ALL MET SEPARATELY AT THE COUNTY JAIL AFTER THE PIETY STREET RAID OF 1970.

HE HAD LEARNED IN 1997 THAT ALBERT AND HERMAN WERE STILL IN ANGOLA AND JOINED THE 1998 DEFENSE MOVEMENT THAT WAS ORGANIZED DURING ALBERT'S THIRD TRIAL.*

HE WOULD LATER TAKE PART IN THE FOUNDING OF THE NATIONAL COALITION TO FREE THE ANGOLA 3.

DO YOU REMEMBER WHEN WE WERE AT ALBERT'S TRIAL IN 1998, ROBERT? YOU WERE CALLED AS A WITNESS.

YES, IT WAS THE FIRST TIME I HAD BEEN IN A ROOM THAT BIG IN THIRTEEN YEARS, A ROOM WITH A WINDOW!

YOU BARELY LOOKED AT ME. YOU STARED OUT THAT WINDOW AS THOUGH TRYING TO ABSORB EVERYTHING THAT YOU COULD SEE BEYOND IT.

I DIDN'T KNOW IF I WOULD EVER LEAVE ANGOLA. IT WAS A CHANCE TO NOURISH MY SPIRIT WITH IMAGES FROM THE OUTSIDE THAT I COULD REMEMBER FOR THE YEARS TO COME.

YOU'RE OUT NOW.

BUT I'LL NEVER BE RID OF ANGOLA, AND ANGOLA ISN'T FREE FROM ME. I DIDN'T SURVIVE ALL OF THIS TO JUST GO TO SLEEP AND BE SILENT. MY TIME THERE IS ETCHED ON MY SOUL.

*ALBERT WAS ONCE AGAIN FOUND GUILTY FOR THE DEATH OF MILLER.

71

IN 1983, I STARTED TO GO BLIND.

I COULDN'T SEE FARTHER THAN A FEW FEET. MY EYES COULD NO LONGER SEE BEYOND THE WALLS OF MY CELL!

AND TODAY, ROBERT?

THERE ARE SOME THINGS THAT WE CAN NEVER GET OVER. I THINK I'LL MOVE ON WITH TIME. I'LL ADJUST TO A CERTAIN EXTENT. BUT NOW I HAVE HIGH BLOOD PRESSURE, NIGHT TERRORS. I'LL NEVER KNOW HOW MUCH DAMAGE THOSE 29 YEARS IN ISOLATION HAVE DONE.

HOW DID YOU KEEP FROM GOING CRAZY?

MALIK, I LIKE TO THINK THAT I STAYED SANE IN SPIRIT. BUT HOW DO YOU GET COVERED IN SHIT WITHOUT COMING OUT STINKING? THE ONLY THING I KNOW IS THAT IN ISOLATION YOUR BRAIN CONTRACTS AND IT CAN BE WITHSTOOD.

TO TELL THE TRUTH, IN A 20-FT. CELL, EVERYTHING SHRINKS, AND EVERY MOMENT IS A BATTLE TO KEEP YOURSELF FROM DISAPPEARING, FROM LOSING YOUR HUMANITY. BUT NOT EVERYONE HAS THE STRENGTH FOR THAT.

A LOT OF THE INMATES LOSE CONTROL. SOME OF THEM ALREADY HAVE MENTAL HEALTH ISSUES WHEN THEY ARE PLACED IN ISOLATION.

PROLONGED ISOLATION CAN TOTALLY ROB SOMEONE OF THEIR OWN IDENTITY, AND I CAN'T SAY AT WHAT POINT I MYSELF REACHED MY EMOTIONAL AND MENTAL LIMIT.

IF I HADN'T BEEN CARRIED BY THE STRENGTH OF MY POLITICAL CONVICTIONS AND THE DESIRE TO HAVE OUR CASES BE HEARD, I MIGHT HAVE GONE CRAZY, AND I DEFINITELY WOULDN'T HAVE SURVIVED.

GOOD MORNING, MR. WALLACE!

IT'S A BEAUTIFUL DAY BUT SO HOT! COULD MY BULL HAVE A DRINK OF WATER?

OF COURSE, MY DEAR FELLOW! DON'T LET THIS POOR ANIMAL DIE OF THIRST!

WELL, WELL, HE CERTAINLY WAS THIRSTY! THIS IS A GOOD-LOOKING ANIMAL YOU GOT HERE!

THANK YOU. AND YOU HAVE A MAGNIFICENT HOME, MR. WALLACE!

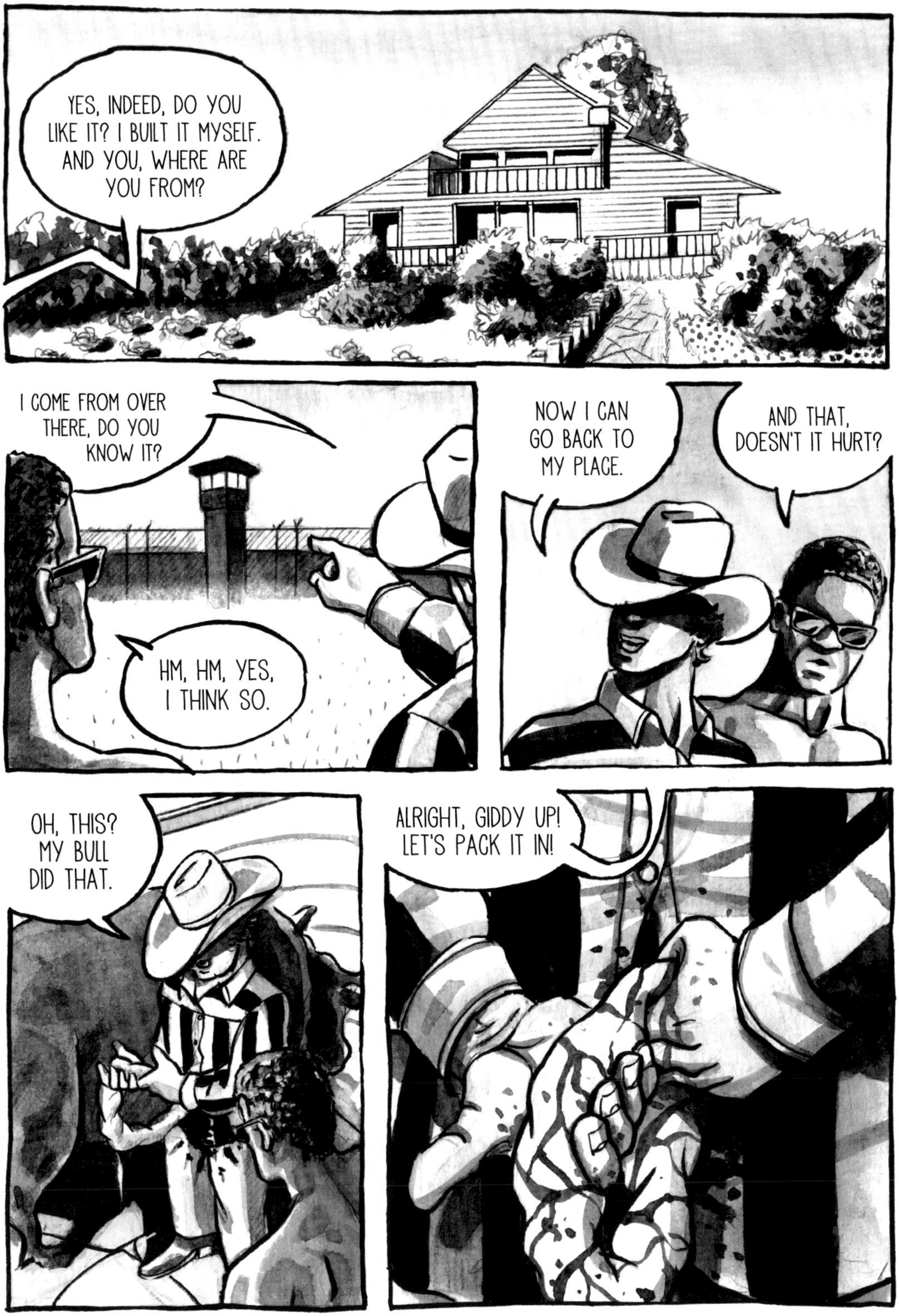
YES, INDEED, DO YOU LIKE IT? I BUILT IT MYSELF. AND YOU, WHERE ARE YOU FROM?
I COME FROM OVER THERE, DO YOU KNOW IT?
HM, HM, YES, I THINK SO.
NOW I CAN GO BACK TO MY PLACE.
AND THAT, DOESN'T IT HURT?
OH, THIS? MY BULL DID THAT.
ALRIGHT, GIDDY UP! LET'S PACK IT IN!

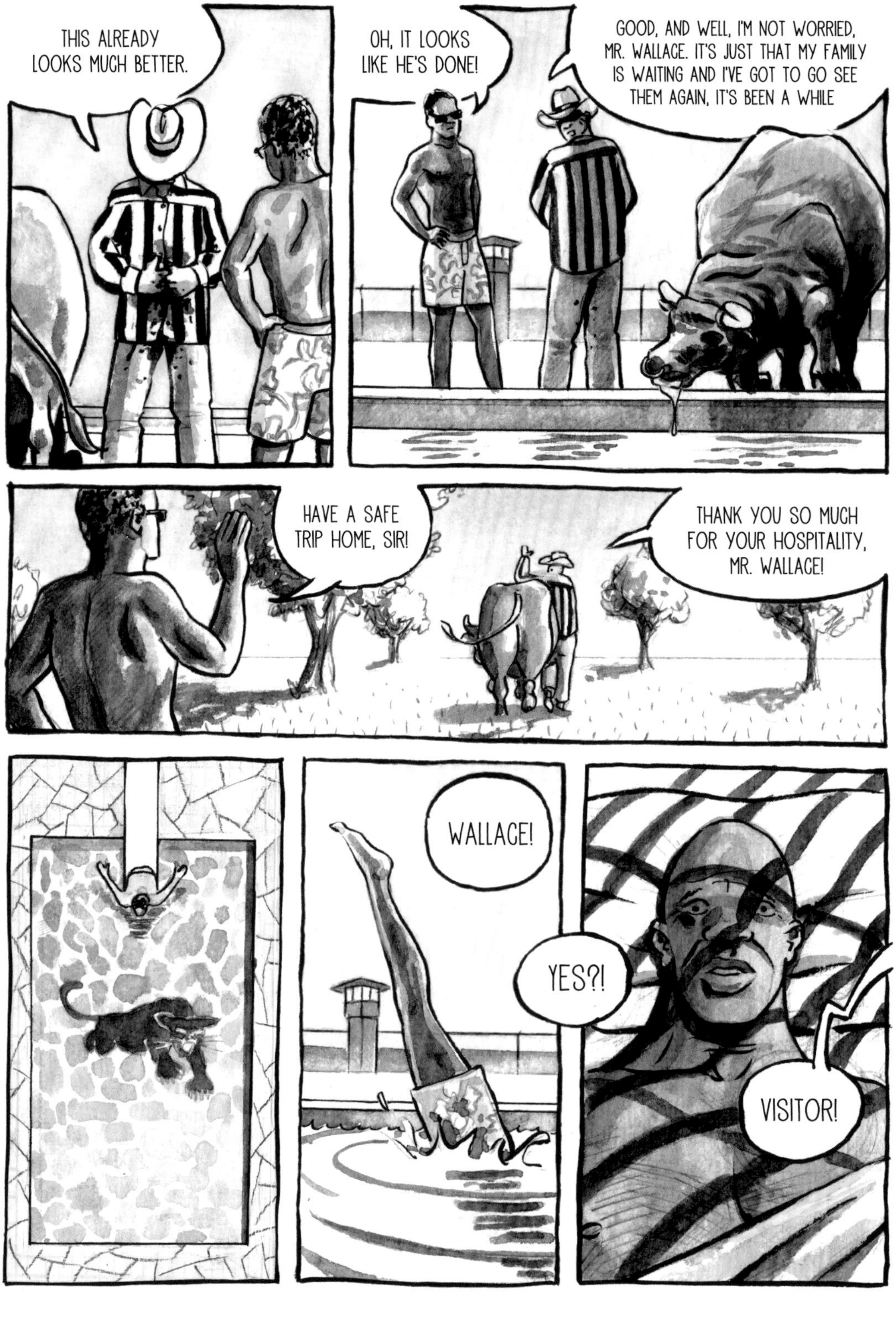
THIS ALREADY LOOKS MUCH BETTER.
OH, IT LOOKS LIKE HE'S DONE!
GOOD, AND WELL, I'M NOT WORRIED, MR. WALLACE. IT'S JUST THAT MY FAMILY IS WAITING AND I'VE GOT TO GO SEE THEM AGAIN, IT'S BEEN A WHILE
HAVE A SAFE TRIP HOME, SIR!
THANK YOU SO MUCH FOR YOUR HOSPITALITY, MR. WALLACE!
WALLACE!
YES?!
VISITOR!

I HAVE SOME GOOD NEWS, HERMAN, BUT TELL ME, FIRST OFF, HOW ARE YOU DOING?

HM, WELL CAN YOU REMIND ME OF WHAT YEAR WE'RE IN? 1998, RIGHT? ALRIGHT, SO YOU WANT AN UPDATE ON THE HEALTH OF A MAN WHO HAS BEEN LOCKED UP IN A 20-FT. CELL SINCE 1972? WHAT SHOULD I START WITH? MY ARTHRITIS, MY HYPERTENSION, MY INSOMNIA, MY STRESS?

NO, THANKS. FORGET ABOUT IT, SCOTT.* TELL ME YOUR GOOD NEWS INSTEAD!

WELL, I TOOK A CLOSE LOOK AT EVERYTHING. FIRST OF ALL, YOU AND ALBERT WERE TRIED SEPARATELY, BEFORE TWO DIFFERENT JURIES, AND THE PROSECUTION DIDN'T USE THE SAME SOURCES OF INFORMATION FOR BOTH TRIALS. SOME OF THE WITNESS ACCOUNTS THAT WERE RELIED ON IN ALBERT'S TRIAL DO NOT EVEN MENTION YOU, AND VICE VERSA.

FURTHERMORE, THESE ACCOUNTS ARE INCOHERENT AND THE EVENTS DESCRIBED IMPOSSIBLE, ESPECIALLY PAUL FOBB'S. HE WAS AN INMATE WHO CLAIMED TO HAVE SEEN ALBERT ENTER THE DORMITORY ALONE WHEN THE MURDER TOOK PLACE. THE STORY HE TOLD IN '73 JUST DOESN'T ADD UP, AND WE NOW KNOW THAT HE WAS PRACTICALLY BLIND, AS WELL AS MENTALLY DISABLED AND A SOCIOPATH WITH A VARIETY OF PERSONALITY DISORDERS.

* SCOTT IS A LAW STUDENT ACTIVIST.

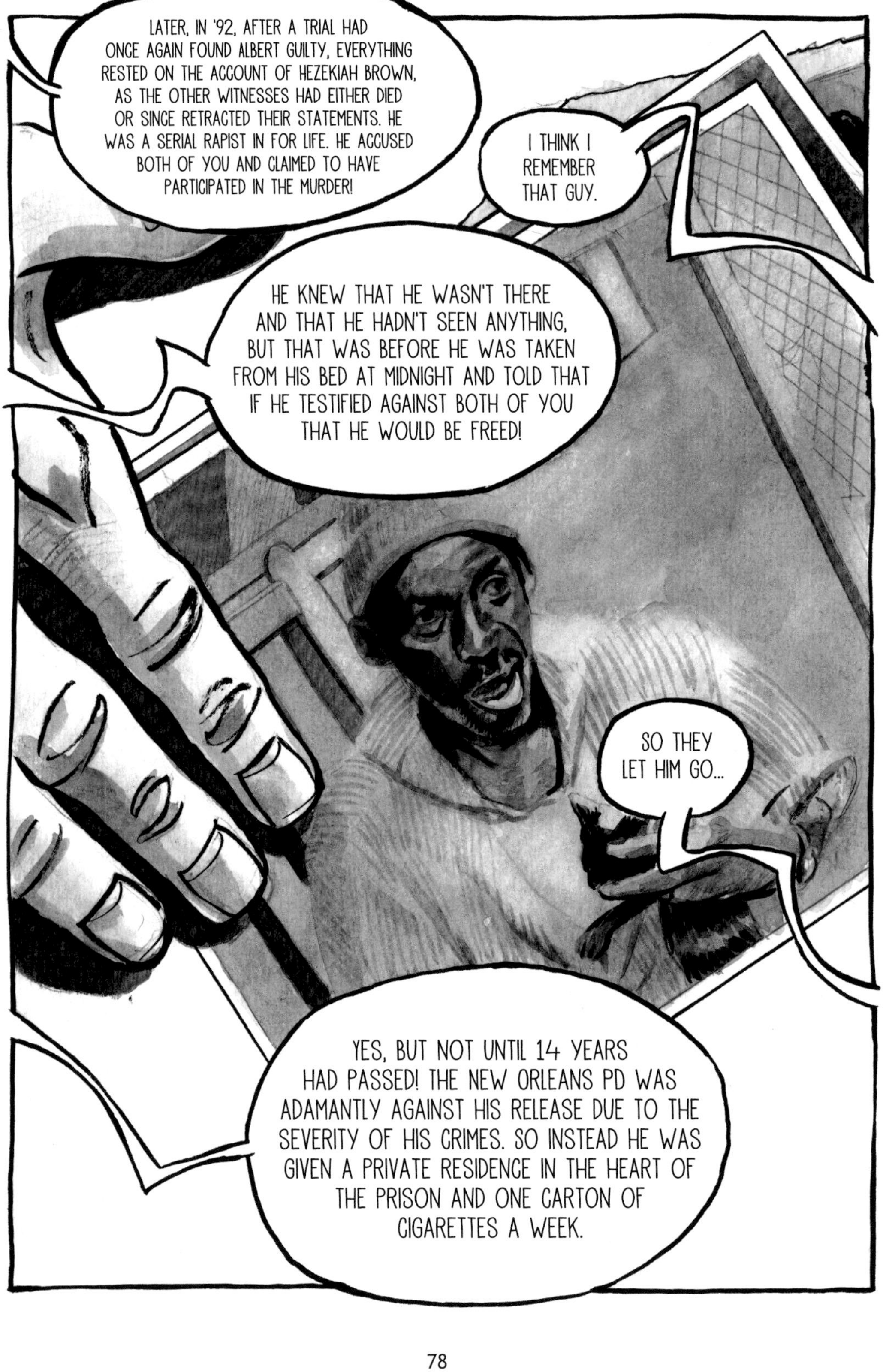
LATER, IN '92, AFTER A TRIAL HAD ONCE AGAIN FOUND ALBERT GUILTY, EVERYTHING RESTED ON THE ACCOUNT OF HEZEKIAH BROWN, AS THE OTHER WITNESSES HAD EITHER DIED OR SINCE RETRACTED THEIR STATEMENTS. HE WAS A SERIAL RAPIST IN FOR LIFE. HE ACCUSED BOTH OF YOU AND CLAIMED TO HAVE PARTICIPATED IN THE MURDER!
I THINK I REMEMBER THAT GUY.
HE KNEW THAT HE WASN'T THERE AND THAT HE HADN'T SEEN ANYTHING, BUT THAT WAS BEFORE HE WAS TAKEN FROM HIS BED AT MIDNIGHT AND TOLD THAT IF HE TESTIFIED AGAINST BOTH OF YOU THAT HE WOULD BE FREED!
SO THEY LET HIM GO...
YES, BUT NOT UNTIL 14 YEARS HAD PASSED! THE NEW ORLEANS PD WAS ADAMANTLY AGAINST HIS RELEASE DUE TO THE SEVERITY OF HIS CRIMES. SO INSTEAD HE WAS GIVEN A PRIVATE RESIDENCE IN THE HEART OF THE PRISON AND ONE CARTON OF CIGARETTES A WEEK.

AND NOW, FOR THE ONLY REAL PHYSICAL EVIDENCE AT THE TRIAL.

REAL BUT WITH A CAVEAT, AS THE TRIAL PROVED THAT THE FINGERPRINTS DIDN'T MATCH MINE, OR ALBERT'S, OR ANY OF THE OTHER SUSPECTS' PRINTS.

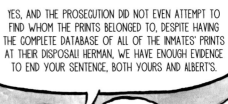

YES, AND THE PROSECUTION DID NOT EVEN ATTEMPT TO FIND WHOM THE PRINTS BELONGED TO, DESPITE HAVING THE COMPLETE DATABASE OF ALL OF THE INMATES' PRINTS AT THEIR DISPOSAL! HERMAN, WE HAVE ENOUGH EVIDENCE TO END YOUR SENTENCE, BOTH YOURS AND ALBERT'S.

THE FINGERPRINT SHOULD BE ENOUGH.

THEY LOST IT.

DAMN, IT'S BEEN AGES. WHAT EVER HAPPENED TO THAT PIECE OF SHIT CHESTER JACKSON?

DEAD, ALL OF THEM, EVEN BROWN.

I HAVE MORE CONFIDENCE IN YOU THAN ALL THE OTHER LAWYERS THAT HAVE PASSED THROUGH HERE.

I READ HUNDREDS OF LETTERS FROM INMATES ASKING THE NATIONAL LAWYERS GUILD FOR HELP. YOURS STOOD APART FROM THE REST, AND I WAS IMMEDIATELY INTRIGUED BY YOUR CASE. WHEN I HEARD YOU AND ALBERT I BELIEVED WHAT YOU SAID. THAT'S ALL.

WE HIRED OTHER LAWYERS AND ALL THEY DID WAS SABOTAGE OUR CASE. YOU'VE BEEN DRIVING FROM OAKLAND TO HERE AND BACK AGAIN, ON YOUR TIME AND AT YOUR PERSONAL EXPENSE. I DON'T CARE THAT YOU HAVEN'T PASSED THE BAR YET.

YOU ARE OUR LAWYER.

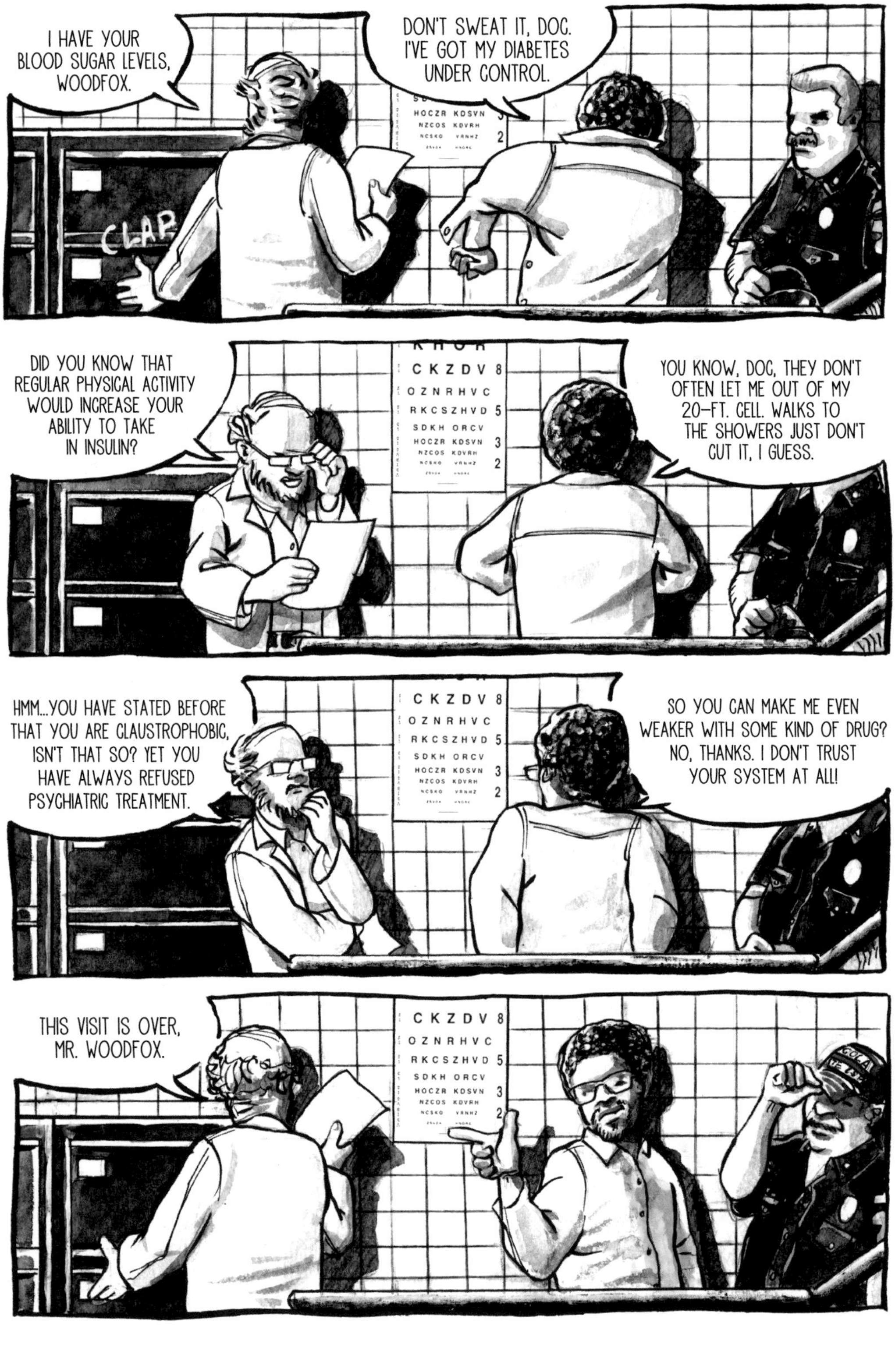
I HAVE YOUR BLOOD SUGAR LEVELS, WOODFOX.
DON'T SWEAT IT, DOC. I'VE GOT MY DIABETES UNDER CONTROL.
DID YOU KNOW THAT REGULAR PHYSICAL ACTIVITY WOULD INCREASE YOUR ABILITY TO TAKE IN INSULIN?
YOU KNOW, DOC, THEY DON'T OFTEN LET ME OUT OF MY 20-FT. CELL. WALKS TO THE SHOWERS JUST DON'T CUT IT, I GUESS.
HMM...YOU HAVE STATED BEFORE THAT YOU ARE CLAUSTROPHOBIC, ISN'T THAT SO? YET YOU HAVE ALWAYS REFUSED PSYCHIATRIC TREATMENT.
SO YOU CAN MAKE ME EVEN WEAKER WITH SOME KIND OF DRUG? NO, THANKS. I DON'T TRUST YOUR SYSTEM AT ALL!
THIS VISIT IS OVER, MR. WOODFOX.

POORLY DEFENDED TILL THE END OF THE 1990S, HERMAN NEVER SUCCEEDED IN DENOUNCING THE CORRUPTION SURROUNDING HIS TRIAL AND THE TESTIMONIES AGAINST HIM.

IN 1972, CHESTER JACKSON AGREED TO ACCUSE HERMAN AND ALBERT FOR A MURDER CHARGE WITH A LIGHTER SENTENCE, 22 YEARS OF FORCED LABOR INSTEAD OF LIFE IN PRISON.

MEANWHILE, HEZEKIAH BROWN GROSSLY BENEFITED FROM A SYSTEM BASED ON FAVORS AND THE PROMISE OF FREEDOM.

FOR THESE REASONS, WHILE BEING DEFENDED BY SCOTT FLEMING AND NICK TRENTICOSTA, ALBERT SAW A JUDICIAL COMMISSION RECOMMEND HIS RELEASE IN 2006.

THE RELEASE WAS DENIED BY THE SUPREME COURT OF LOUISIANA WITHOUT COMMENT OR ARGUMENT.

FOR ME, EVERYTHING TOOK OFF IN 2001.

KING, PHONE!

HEY, CHRIS!

UHUH... YEAH IT'S OK.

WHAT?! IN ONE WEEK? BUT, THAT... THAT'S AMAZING, CHRIS!

HUH? A PROTEST? WHAT KIND OF PROTEST?

NO, CHRIS, I CAN'T... HUH? WELL, AFTER ALL, YOU'RE THE LAWYER... OK, IN ONE WEEK.

OK, BYE, CHRIS!

SO, THE OL' VETERAN GOT SOME GOOD NEWS?

HUH, YEAH, COULD BE, GUARD... COULD BE.

FEBRUARY 8TH, 2001

MY LAWYER, CHRIS ABERLE, CONVINCED THE STATE THAT MY CONSTITUTIONAL RIGHT TO A JURY OF MY PEERS HAD NOT BEEN RESPECTED.

IN FACT, THE 1975 TRIAL THAT SENTENCED ME TO LIFE A SECOND TIME WASN'T FAIR: THE JURY WAS MADE UP OF ONLY WHITE MEN, AND SOME OF THEM WORKED AT THE PRISON!

IT WAS OUT OF THE QUESTION THAT THE STATE WOULD ACKNOWLEDGE THE TRIAL'S LACK OF CREDIBILITY. BUT CHRIS HAD SUCCEEDED IN PROVING THAT WOMEN WERE EXCLUDED FROM THE JURY. IT WAS VOTED ON AND DECIDED THAT A NEW TRIAL WOULD BE HELD.

CHRIS ALSO DEMONSTRATED THAT MY VERDICT WAS BASED ON THE ACCOUNTS OF TWO UNTRUSTWORTHY INMATES, ONE OF WHOM HAD ALREADY RETRACTED HIS STATEMENT.

FACED WITH PROOF OF THE TRIAL'S ABERRATIONS, THE STATE PROPOSED A DEAL.

WE WILL APPEAR BEFORE THE STATE COURT AND ASK THAT THIS SENTENCE BE LIFTED IF HE PLEADS GUILTY TO A LESSER CRIME.

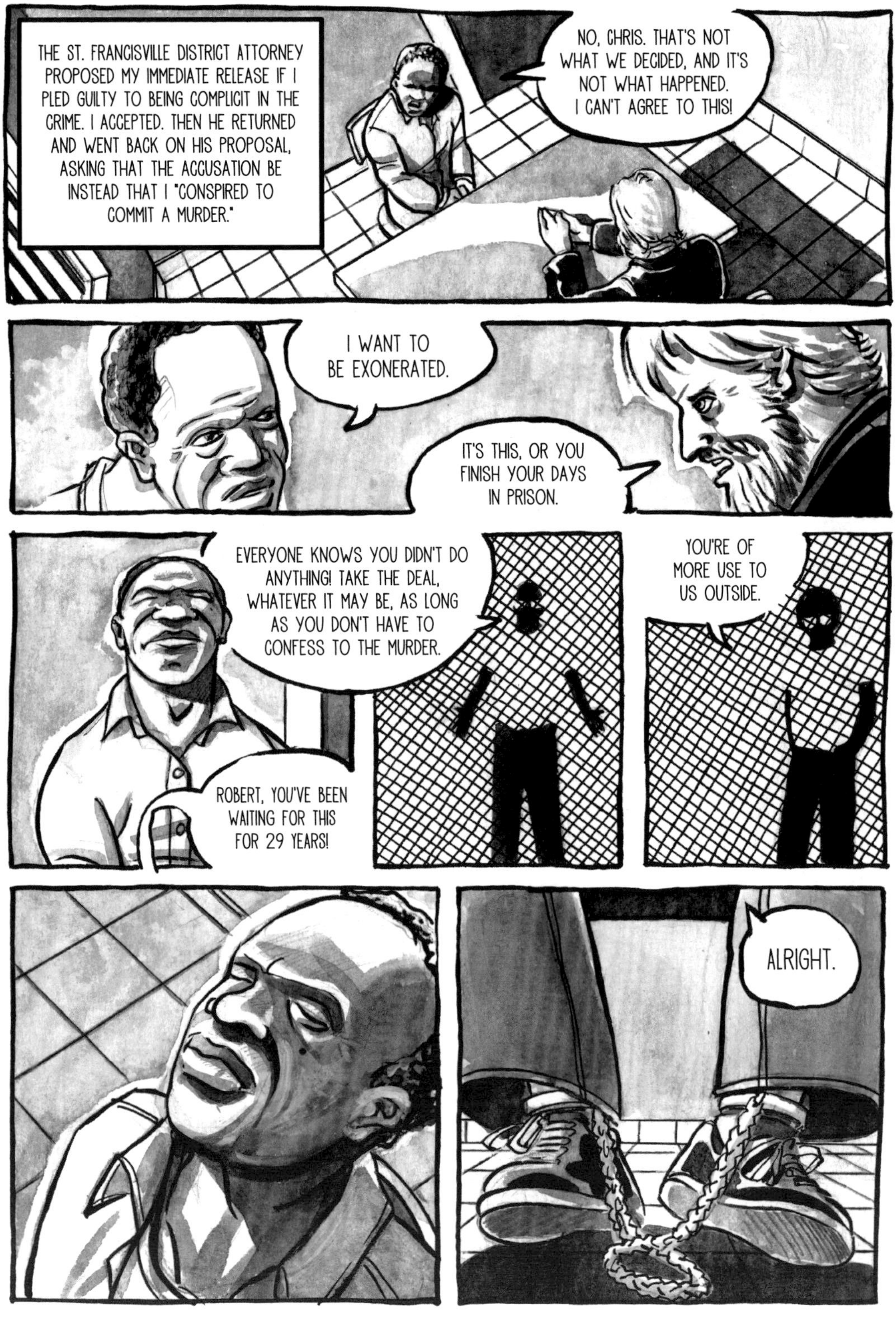
THE ST. FRANCISVILLE DISTRICT ATTORNEY PROPOSED MY IMMEDIATE RELEASE IF I PLED GUILTY TO BEING COMPLICIT IN THE CRIME. I ACCEPTED. THEN HE RETURNED AND WENT BACK ON HIS PROPOSAL, ASKING THAT THE ACCUSATION BE INSTEAD THAT I "CONSPIRED TO COMMIT A MURDER."
NO, CHRIS. THAT'S NOT WHAT WE DECIDED, AND IT'S NOT WHAT HAPPENED. I CAN'T AGREE TO THIS!
I WANT TO BE EXONERATED.
IT'S THIS, OR YOU FINISH YOUR DAYS IN PRISON.
EVERYONE KNOWS YOU DIDN'T DO ANYTHING! TAKE THE DEAL, WHATEVER IT MAY BE, AS LONG AS YOU DON'T HAVE TO CONFESS TO THE MURDER.
ROBERT, YOU'VE BEEN WAITING FOR THIS FOR 29 YEARS!
YOU'RE OF MORE USE TO US OUTSIDE.
ALRIGHT.

RAISE YOUR HAND AND SAY, "I SWEAR!"

THE RIGHT? THE LEFT?

THE LEFT!

I SWEAR!

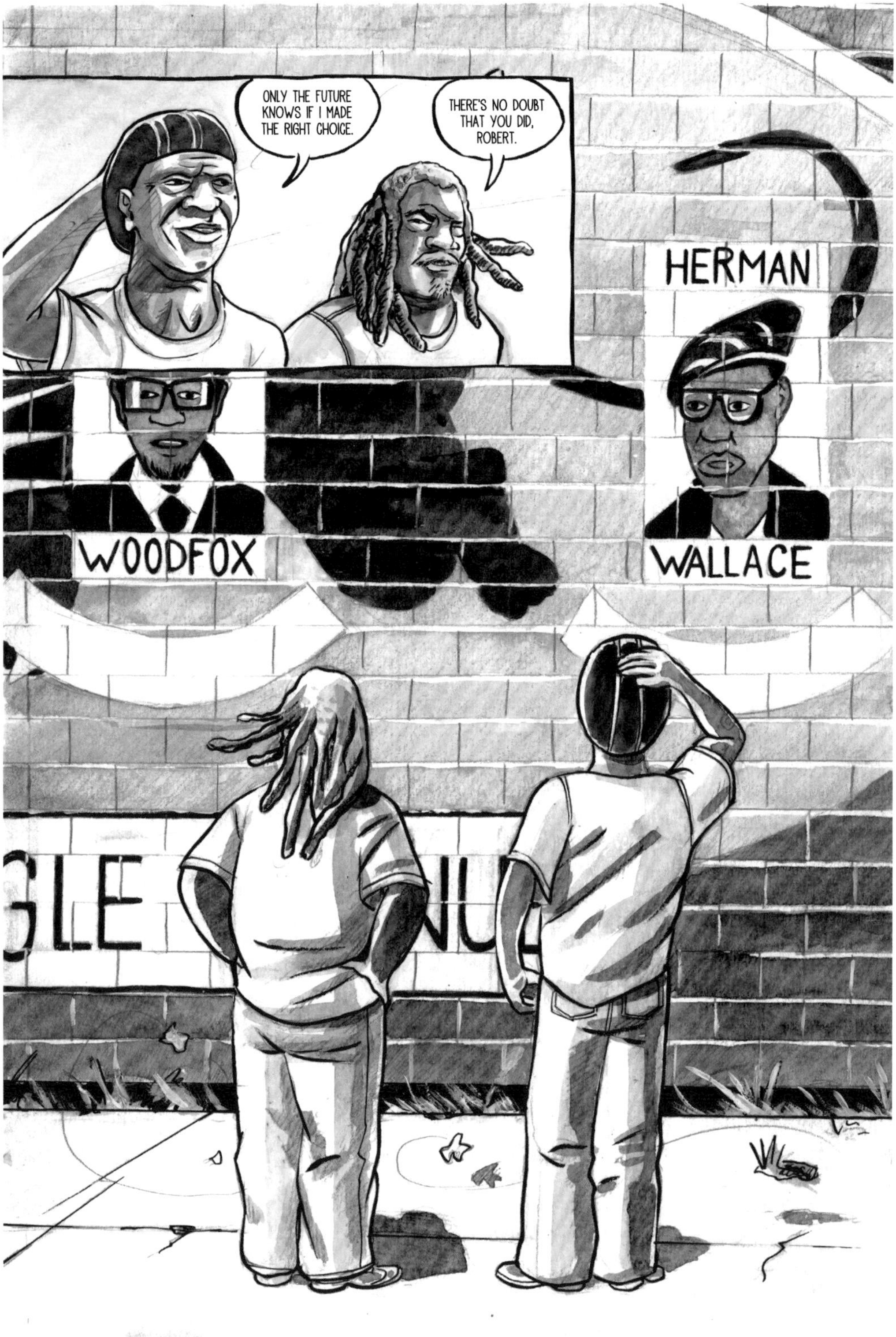
ONLY THE FUTURE KNOWS IF I MADE THE RIGHT CHOICE.
THERE'S NO DOUBT THAT YOU DID, ROBERT.
HERMAN
WOODFOX
WALLACE
GLE
NU

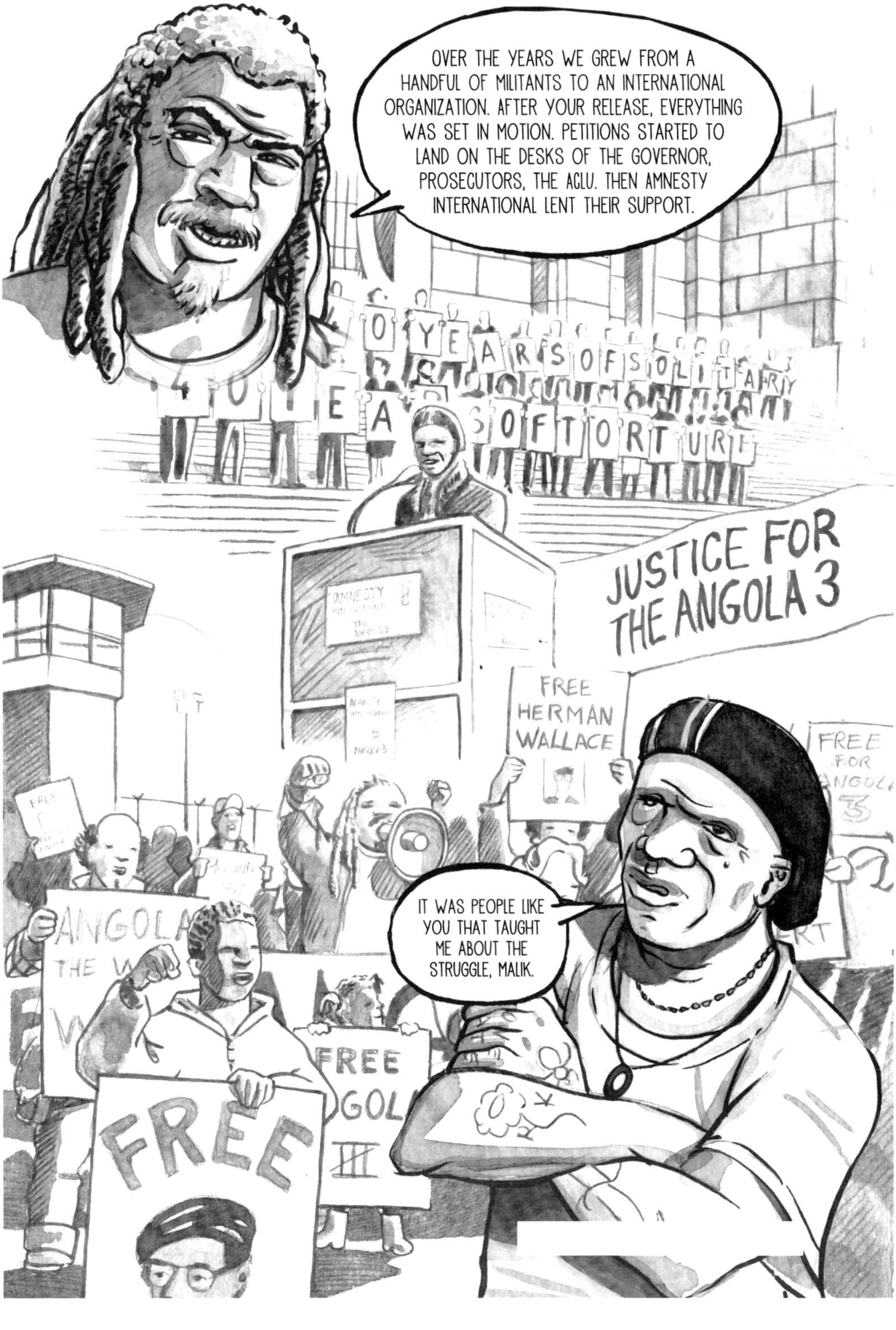
OVER THE YEARS WE GREW FROM A HANDFUL OF MILITANTS TO AN INTERNATIONAL ORGANIZATION. AFTER YOUR RELEASE, EVERYTHING WAS SET IN MOTION. PETITIONS STARTED TO LAND ON THE DESKS OF THE GOVERNOR, PROSECUTORS, THE ACLU. THEN AMNESTY INTERNATIONAL LENT THEIR SUPPORT.
JUSTICE FOR THE ANGOLA 3
FREE HERMAN WALLACE
IT WAS PEOPLE LIKE YOU THAT TAUGHT ME ABOUT THE STRUGGLE, MALIK.
FREE

I TRAVELED THE WORLD TO SHARE THE STORY OF MY TWO FRIENDS.

I MET ALL THOSE WHO WOULD HEAR ME SPEAK, EVEN DESMOND TUTU IN SOUTH AFRICA.

THEN CAME THE DOCUMENTARIES, THE VIDEOS SHARED ONLINE.

In the land of the free...

3 men, 100 years in solitary confinement. In América Today.

Narrated by SAMUEL L. JACKSON

"See this film because they can't"

THE ANGOLA 3 BECAME ONE OF THE MOST POWERFUL SYMBOLS OF THE BROKEN JUSTICE SYSTEM AND THE NEED FOR PRISON REFORM.

THE YEAR I WAS RELEASED, THE ACLU HELPED ME FILE A SUIT. WE DENOUNCED THE DEHUMANIZING PRACTICE OF PROLONGED CONFINEMENT IN ISOLATION. WE DID IT FOR HERMAN AND ALBERT, BUT ALSO FOR ALL OF THE OTHER INMATES SUFFERING IN ISOLATION IN AMERICAN PRISONS.

NICK TRENTICOSTA, ONE OF ALBERT AND HERMAN'S LAWYERS, WAS AT OUR SIDE.

WALLACE AND WOODFOX HAVE SEEN THEIR CASES EXAMINED EVERY 90 DAYS BY A COMMITTEE THAT IS SUPPOSED TO DETERMINE WHETHER THEY SHOULD REMAIN IN ISOLATION. THE VERDICT IS THE SAME EVERY TIME.

THE COMMITTEE MAINTAINS THEIR ISOLATION BASED ON "THE NATURE OF THE INITIAL INFRACTION."

EVEN IF YOU BELIEVE THAT IT SHOULD BE LEGAL TO DETAIN SOMEONE IN ISOLATION FOR THIRTY YEARS, YOU MUST PROVE AT EACH HEARING THAT YOUR DECISION IS JUSTIFIED, THAT YOU HAVE JUST REASONS FOR LEAVING THEM WHERE THEY ARE. SO, IF YOU LOOK AT THE PRISON'S RECORDS,

THESE MEN, YES, THEY ARE PRISONERS, BUT THEY HAVE NOT DONE A SINGLE THING DURING THE PAST THIRTY YEARS TO JUSTIFY THAT THEY REMAIN IN ISOLATION.

THE COMMITTEE THAT MEETS EVERY NINETY DAYS IS A DISGRACE!

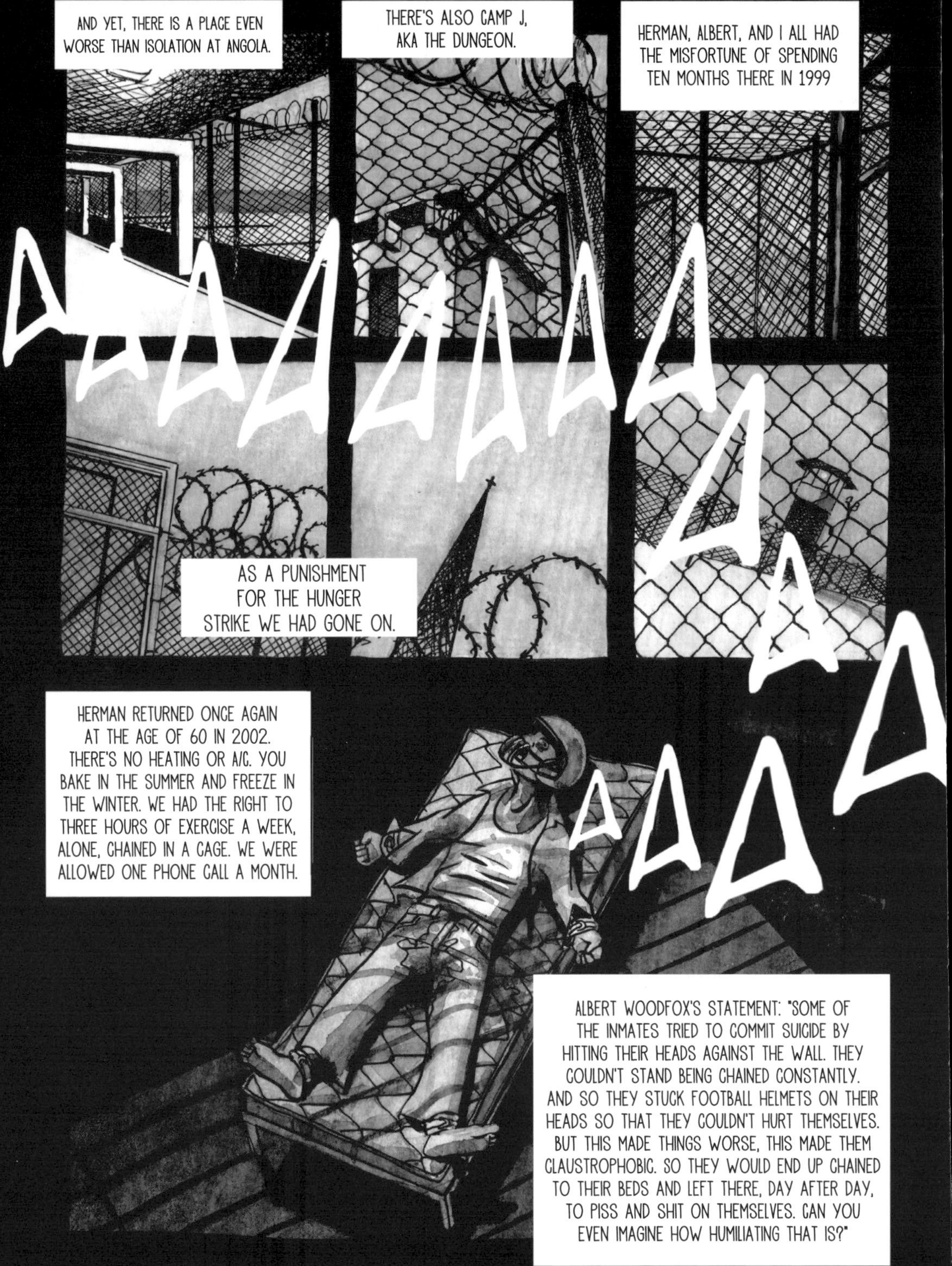
AND YET, THERE IS A PLACE EVEN WORSE THAN ISOLATION AT ANGOLA.
THERE'S ALSO CAMP J, AKA THE DUNGEON.
HERMAN, ALBERT, AND I ALL HAD THE MISFORTUNE OF SPENDING TEN MONTHS THERE IN 1999
AS A PUNISHMENT FOR THE HUNGER STRIKE WE HAD GONE ON.
AAAAAAAAAAAAAAAAA
HERMAN RETURNED ONCE AGAIN AT THE AGE OF 60 IN 2002. THERE'S NO HEATING OR A/C. YOU BAKE IN THE SUMMER AND FREEZE IN THE WINTER. WE HAD THE RIGHT TO THREE HOURS OF EXERCISE A WEEK, ALONE, CHAINED IN A CAGE. WE WERE ALLOWED ONE PHONE CALL A MONTH.
ALBERT WOODFOX'S STATEMENT: "SOME OF THE INMATES TRIED TO COMMIT SUICIDE BY HITTING THEIR HEADS AGAINST THE WALL. THEY COULDN'T STAND BEING CHAINED CONSTANTLY. AND SO THEY STUCK FOOTBALL HELMETS ON THEIR HEADS SO THAT THEY COULDN'T HURT THEMSELVES. BUT THIS MADE THINGS WORSE, THIS MADE THEM CLAUSTROPHOBIC. SO THEY WOULD END UP CHAINED TO THEIR BEDS AND LEFT THERE, DAY AFTER DAY, TO PISS AND SHIT ON THEMSELVES. CAN YOU EVEN IMAGINE HOW HUMILIATING THAT IS?"

IN MARCH 2008, FOLLOWING A VISIT TO ANGOLA BY MEMBERS OF CONGRESS, HERMAN AND ALBERT WERE BOTH TRANSFERRED TO A HIGH SECURITY UNIT THAT HELD ONLY 20 INMATES. UNDER THE PRETENSE THAT THEY WERE BEING PUNISHED FOR MINOR INFRACTIONS, THEY WERE ONCE AGAIN PLACED IN ISOLATION 8 MONTHS LATER, THEN TRANSFERRED TO SEPARATE PENITENTIARIES, WHERE THEY CONTINUED TO LIVE IN ISOLATION.

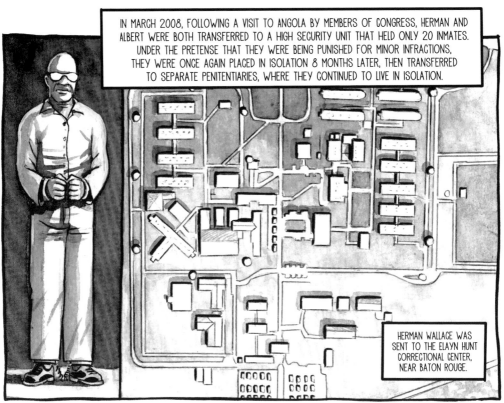

HERMAN WALLACE WAS SENT TO THE ELAYN HUNT CORRECTIONAL CENTER, NEAR BATON ROUGE.

AND ALBERT WOODFOX WAS SENT TO THE DAVID WADE CORRECTIONAL CENTER, WHICH IS LOCATED IN THE NORTHERNMOST PART OF LOUISIANA, ROUGHLY 6 HOURS AWAY FROM NEW ORLEANS, WHICH MADE VISITS FROM HIS FAMILY AND FRIENDS EVEN MORE DIFFICULT.

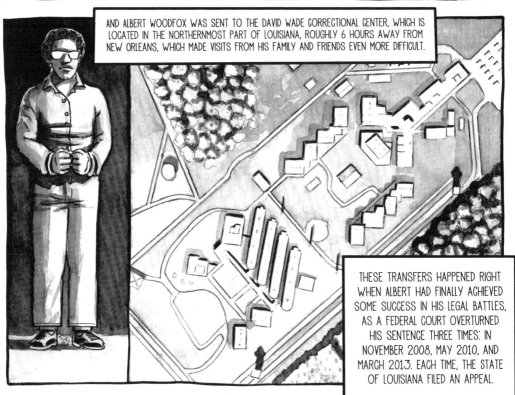

THESE TRANSFERS HAPPENED RIGHT WHEN ALBERT HAD FINALLY ACHIEVED SOME SUCCESS IN HIS LEGAL BATTLES, AS A FEDERAL COURT OVERTURNED HIS SENTENCE THREE TIMES: IN NOVEMBER 2008, MAY 2010, AND MARCH 2013. EACH TIME, THE STATE OF LOUISIANA FILED AN APPEAL.

ON OCTOBER 22ND, 2008, BURL CAIN AND HIS LAWYERS APPEARED BEFORE THE BATON ROUGE ATTORNEY GENERAL IN HIS OFFICE, TO DISCUSS THE COMPLAINT FILED BY ALBERT WOODFOX REGARDING HIS PERPETUAL DETENTION IN ISOLATION.

NICK TRENTICOSTA, WOODFOX'S LAWYER, REPRESENTED HIS CLIENT.

GOOD AFTERNOON WARDEN CAIN. HOW ARE YOU?

FINE.

WARDEN CAIN, YOU KNOW WHY YOU'RE HERE TODAY, DON'T YOU?

I DO.

AND HAVE WE MET AND DISCUSSED THIS CASE?

WE HAVE.

WARDEN CAIN, YOU PREVIOUSLY GAVE A DEPOSITION IN A CIVIL MATTER THAT'S CONNECTED—A CIVIL MATTER INVOLVING ALBERT WOODFOX; IS THAT CORRECT?

RIGHT.

AND WAS THAT DEPOSITION GIVEN ON NOVEMBER 30TH, 2006?

IT WAS.

ALL RIGHT. WE ARE GOING TO REFER TO THAT DEPOSITION IF IT IS OKAY WITH YOU, WARDEN CAIN, AS CAIN'S DEPOSITION ONE?

OKAY.

SO THAT THERE WILL BE CLARITY, IN THAT DEPOSITION, DID YOU DESCRIBE ALBERT WOODFOX AS QUOTE, "MODEL PRISONER?"

I DID IN A SMALL, CONFINED DESCRIPTION OF HIS ENVIRONMENT WHAT HE IS AT THAT PARTICULAR SNAPSHOT TIME. IT WAS NOT ALL-ENCOMPASSING.

OKAY. WELL, FIRST OF ALL, GIVE US THE DEFINITION. WHAT IS YOUR DEFINITION OF A MODEL PRISONER?

WELL, A TRUE MODEL PRISONER IS SOMEONE WHO HAS BEEN MORALLY REHABILITATED, AND WHO, YOU KNOW, THAT YOU CAN TRUST TO LIVE AND WORK AND MOVE AND WORK AMONG ANYBODY.

OKAY. DO YOU FEEL—

IN PRISON.

DO YOU FEEL THAT DEFINITION FITS ALBERT WOODFOX?

ABSOLUTELY NOT.

WELL, TELL ME WHAT FACTORS WOULD YOU TAKE INTO CONSIDERATION TO DETERMINE WHETHER SOMEBODY WAS A QUOTE, "MODEL PRISONER?"

WELL, NUMBER ONE IS, HE IS NOT A RULE VIOLATOR, BUT A RULE FOLLOWER, AND SOMEONE WHO GOES WITH THE FLOW AS FAR AS WHAT IS RIGHT AND WHAT IS WRONG, AND DOESN'T DO WHAT IS WRONG, AND SOMEONE WHO PARTICIPATES IN PROGRAMS MORALLY; AND BY THAT, I MEAN I'M TALKING ABOUT FOR INSTANCE, AN EXAMPLE WOULD BE LIKE HOSPICE CAREGIVERS, ACTIVE IN CHURCH, ACTIVE IN CLUBS AND ORGANIZATIONS, AND NOT LOOKING OUT TO SELF AND FOR SELF GAIN, BUT LOOKING OUT FOR THE GOOD OF ALL LIKE WE DO AS CITIZENS. WE CARE ABOUT EACH OTHER AND WE SHARE AND WE GIVE. WE'RE NOT TAKERS

OKAY.

BUT MORAL— A MORAL PERSON.

ALL RIGHT. IN DETERMINING WHETHER SOMEONE IS MORALLY REHABILITATED, AND WHETHER THEY ARE A MODEL PRISONER, WOULD YOU WANT TO KNOW THEIR COMPLETE DISCIPLINARY HISTORY?

WELL, YOU WOULD.

OKAY. DID YOU HAVE AN OPPORTUNITY TO REVIEW THAT HISTORY PRIOR TO GIVING YOUR NOVEMBER 30TH, 2006, DEPOSITION?

I REALLY DIDN'T. I HADN'T REVIEWED THAT ALL TOO MUCH.

OKAY. HAVE YOU HAD AN OPPORTUNITY TO DO THAT FOR TODAY'S DEPOSITION?

I HAVE.

AND DO YOU HAVE RECORDS IN FRONT OF YOU REFLECTING ALBERT WOODFOX'S DISCIPLINARY HISTORY?

I DO.

WHEN WAS HIS LAST— STARTING NOW AND GOING BACKWARDS, WHEN WAS HE LAST DISCIPLINED AT ANGOLA?

HIS LAST ACTUAL DISCIPLINARY REPORT WAS 5/16/08 FOR PORNOGRAPHY, WHICH WAS IN MAY OF THIS YEAR AFTER HE MOVED TO THE OTHER DORM.

OKAY.

HE HAD FIVE PAGES OF PORNOGRAPHY, WHICH IS AGAINST THE RULES AT ANGOLA. HE HAD THREE OTHER INFRACTIONS THAT WE DIDN'T WRITE HIM UP FOR, AND ONE IS HE DID THE THREE-WAY PHONE CALLS, AND DID AN INTERVIEW WITH THE PRESS WHICH IS ABSOLUTELY ILLEGAL AT ANGOLA.

AND ALSO THEN HE AND HERMAN WALLACE SWAPPED THEIR PHONE ID NUMBERS, PIN NUMBERS—YOU KNOW, TALKING—CALLING LAWYERS AND THINGS LIKE THAT...

WE DON'T ALLOW INMATES TO DO INTERVIEWS WITH THE PRESS UNLESS I PERSONALLY APPROVE IT, OR IT'S PART OF SOMETHING TO REHABILITATE, TO PROJECT ANGOLA'S POSITIVE SIDE OR PROJECT THE TRUTH.

...FOR THOSE INFRACTIONS, WE DIDN'T WRITE HIM UP...

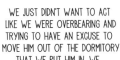

WHY NOT?

HUM...

WELL, WE DIDN'T WANT TO LOOK LIKE WE WERE NITPICKY.

WE JUST DIDN'T WANT TO ACT LIKE WE WERE OVERBEARING AND TRYING TO HAVE AN EXCUSE TO MOVE HIM OUT OF THE DORMITORY THAT WE PUT HIM IN. WE WERE TRYING TO ACT IN GOOD FAITH.

AND SO ALSO, WE WERE KIND OF CURIOUS TO SEE JUST HOW FAR THEY WOULD GO. AND SO—JUST TO SEE WHAT RULES THEY WOULD BREAK. NOW, THE PORNOGRAPHY WE WOULDN'T LET GO. WE HAD TO DO SOMETHING THERE, BECAUSE WE DO NOT ALLOW THAT IN PRISON.

WHY NOT?

WHY IS THAT SUCH A CONCERN TO YOU?

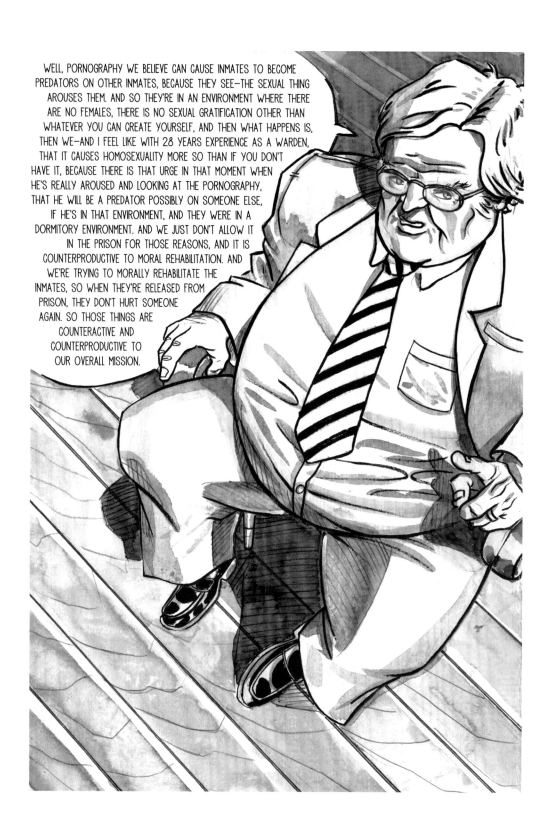

WELL, PORNOGRAPHY WE BELIEVE CAN CAUSE INMATES TO BECOME
PREDATORS ON OTHER INMATES, BECAUSE THEY SEE—THE SEXUAL THING
 AROUSES THEM. AND SO THEY'RE IN AN ENVIRONMENT WHERE THERE
ARE NO FEMALES, THERE IS NO SEXUAL GRATIFICATION OTHER THAN
WHATEVER YOU CAN CREATE YOURSELF, AND THEN WHAT HAPPENS IS,
THEN WE—AND I FEEL LIKE WITH 28 YEARS EXPERIENCE AS A WARDEN,
THAT IT CAUSES HOMOSEXUALITY MORE SO THAN IF YOU DON'T
HAVE IT, BECAUSE THERE IS THAT URGE IN THAT MOMENT WHEN
HE'S REALLY AROUSED AND LOOKING AT THE PORNOGRAPHY,
THAT HE WILL BE A PREDATOR POSSIBLY ON SOMEONE ELSE,
IF HE'S IN THAT ENVIRONMENT, AND THEY WERE IN A
DORMITORY ENVIRONMENT. AND WE JUST DON'T ALLOW IT
IN THE PRISON FOR THOSE REASONS, AND IT IS
COUNTERPRODUCTIVE TO MORAL REHABILITATION. AND
WE'RE TRYING TO MORALLY REHABILITATE THE
INMATES, SO WHEN THEY'RE RELEASED FROM
PRISON, THEY DON'T HURT SOMEONE
AGAIN. SO THOSE THINGS ARE
COUNTERACTIVE AND
COUNTERPRODUCTIVE TO
OUR OVERALL MISSION.

AT THE END OF FEBRUARY 2013, A FEDERAL COURT OVER-TURNED WOODFOX'S SENTENCE FOR THE THIRD TIME, AND ORDERED HIS RELEASE, BASED ON THE OBVIOUS RACIAL DISCRIMINATION OF THE JURY AT HIS 1992 TRIAL. LOUISIANA'S ATTORNEY GENERAL JAMES "BUDDY" CALDWELL WOULDN'T ALLOW THIS TO HAPPEN AND THE STATE FILED AN APPEAL.

THERE ARE NO FLAWS IN OUR EVIDENCE AND THIS CASE IS VERY STRONG.

WE FEEL CONFIDENT

THAT WE WILL AGAIN PREVAIL AT THE FIFTH CIRCUIT COURT OF APPEALS.

HOWEVER, IF WE DO NOT, WE ARE FULLY PREPARED AND WILLING TO RETRY THE MURDERER AGAIN.

BRENT MILLER'S WIDOW, TEENIE ROGERS, WAS 16 YEARS OLD WHEN THEY WERE MARRIED. TWO MONTHS LATER, HER HUSBAND WAS BRUTALLY KILLED WHILE ON DUTY AS A PRISON GUARD IN ANGOLA.

FOR A LONG TIME SHE BELIEVED THAT JUSTICE HAD BEEN SERVED.

YEARS LATER, WHEN SHE WAS MADE AWARE OF THE DISCREPANCIES AND THE TOTAL ABSENCE OF CONCRETE EVIDENCE,

SHE BEGAN TO THINK THAT IF SHE HAD BEEN ON THE JURY THAT SHE WOULD NOT HAVE FOUND WALLACE AND WOODFOX GUILTY. TODAY SHE PUBLICLY STATES THAT SHE NOT ONLY CONSIDERS THEM TO BE INNOCENT, BUT THAT SHE OPPOSED THEIR HORRIFYING TREATMENT.

AFTER PARTICIPATING IN A DOCUMENTARY, SHE EVEN MADE AN APPEAL IN 2014, WITH THE HELP OF AMNESTY INTERNATIONAL, CALLING FOR THE RELEASE OF THE LAST REMAINING INMATE!

IN 2008, AMNESTY INTERNATIONAL MADE THE LIBERATION OF THE ANGOLA 3 ONE OF ITS PRIORITIES. FOR HERMAN, THE URGENCY WAS OF PROFOUND IMPORTANCE, DUE TO HIS AGGRESSIVE CANCER, A DISEASE THAT HAD GONE UNDIAGNOSED UNTIL 2013.

ON JULY 10TH, 2013, HERMAN'S POOR HEALTH AND THE GROWING CAMPAIGN FOR HIS LIBERATION PUT ENOUGH PRESSURE ON THE AUTHORITIES THAT HE WAS MOVED TO A DORMITORY FOR TEN INMATES.

A CAMPAIGN STARTED BY AMNESTY INTERNATIONAL CALLING FOR HIS RELEASE GARNERED OVER 100,000 SIGNATURES. THE STATE OF LOUISIANA FOUGHT IT UNTIL THE VERY END.

THIS WOULD PUT AN END TO HIS 41 YEARS IN ISOLATION.

ON SATURDAY, AUGUST 31ST, I WAS TRANSFERRED TO LSU HOSPITAL FOR EVALUATION. I WAS INFORMED THAT THE CHEMO TREATMENTS HAD FAILED AND WERE MAKING MATTERS WORSE AND SO ALL TREATMENT CAME TO AN END. THE ONCOLOGISTS ADVISED THAT NOTHING CAN BE DONE FOR ME MEDICALLY WITHIN THE STANDARD CARE THAT THEY ARE AUTHORIZED TO PROVIDE. THEY RECOMMENDED THAT I BE ADMITTED TO HOSPICE CARE TO MAKE MY REMAINING DAYS AS COMFORTABLE AS POSSIBLE. I HAVE BEEN GIVEN TWO MONTHS TO LIVE.

I WANT THE WORLD TO KNOW THAT I AM AN INNOCENT MAN AND THAT ALBERT WOODFOX IS INNOCENT AS WELL. WE ARE JUST TWO OF THOUSANDS OF WRONGFULLY CONVICTED PRISONERS HELD CAPTIVE IN THE AMERICAN GULAG. WE MOURN FOR THE FAMILY OF BRENT MILLER AND THE MANY OTHER VICTIMS OF MURDER WHO WILL NEVER BE ABLE TO FIND CLOSURE FOR THE LOSS OF THEIR LOVED ONES DUE THE UNJUST CRIMINAL JUSTICE SYSTEM IN THIS COUNTRY. WE MOURN FOR THE LOSS OF THE FAMILIES OF THOSE UNJUSTLY ACCUSED WHO SUFFER THE LOSS OF THEIR LOVED ONES AS WELL.

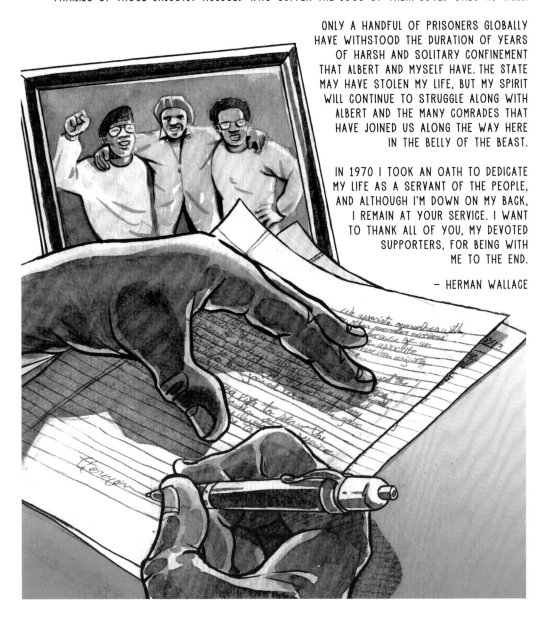

ONLY A HANDFUL OF PRISONERS GLOBALLY HAVE WITHSTOOD THE DURATION OF YEARS OF HARSH AND SOLITARY CONFINEMENT THAT ALBERT AND MYSELF HAVE. THE STATE MAY HAVE STOLEN MY LIFE, BUT MY SPIRIT WILL CONTINUE TO STRUGGLE ALONG WITH ALBERT AND THE MANY COMRADES THAT HAVE JOINED US ALONG THE WAY HERE IN THE BELLY OF THE BEAST.

IN 1970 I TOOK AN OATH TO DEDICATE MY LIFE AS A SERVANT OF THE PEOPLE, AND ALTHOUGH I'M DOWN ON MY BACK, I REMAIN AT YOUR SERVICE. I WANT TO THANK ALL OF YOU, MY DEVOTED SUPPORTERS, FOR BEING WITH ME TO THE END.

– HERMAN WALLACE

OCTOBER 1ST, 2013.
7:30 PM

HUNT CORRECTIONAL CENTER

STOP

WE WILL BEGIN THIS EDITION OF DEMOCRACY NOW! WITH A CASE THAT WE HAVE BEEN FOLLOWING CLOSELY FOR SEVERAL YEARS. HERMAN WALLACE OF THE ANGOLA 3 WAS RELEASED LAST NIGHT AFTER SPENDING OVER 40 YEARS IN ISOLATION. HE WAS TAKEN DIRECTLY TO A HOSPITAL, AND SOON THEREAFTER PASSED AWAY OF TERMINAL LIVER CANCER.

EVERYTHING BEGAN ON TUESDAY, OCTOBER 1ST, WHEN FEDERAL JUDGE JACKSON CALLED FOR HIS SENTENCE TO BE OVERTURNED AND ORDERED HIS IMMEDIATE RELEASE.

AS A LEGAL BATTLE ENSUED BETWEEN JUDGE JACKSON AND THE STATE OF LOUISIANA, HERMAN WALLACE'S LAWYERS SENT AN AMBULANCE TO WAIT FOR HIM AT THE PRISON'S GATES. AT 7:30 PM, HERMAN WALLACE, AT AGE 71, FINALLY LEFT THE PRISON IN AN AMBULANCE THAT TOOK HIM TO A NEW ORLEANS HOSPITAL.

JUDGE JACKSON PRONOUNCED THE OVERTURNING OF HERMAN'S SENTENCE BASED ON THE FACT THAT THERE WERE NO WOMEN ON THE JURY AT THE TIME, AND CALLED FOR HIM TO BE FREED WITHOUT DELAY. BUT THE STATE OF LOUISIANA OPPOSED THIS DECISION.

JACKSON FIRMLY STOOD HIS GROUND AND THREATENED TO FILE A SUIT FOR THE OBSTRUCTION OF JUSTICE IF THE STATE DID NOT FOLLOW HIS ORDERS.

THE STATE ACQUIESCED, BUT THE VERY NEXT DAY DISTRICT ATTORNEY SAMUEL D'AQUILA LAUNCHED AN INQUEST AGAINST HERMAN AND PLANNED TO FORCE HERMAN TO APPEAR BEFORE THE WEST FELICIANA PARISH COURT IN 2014.

I SAY HE IS A MURDERER, AND HE IS NOT INNOCENT. THE CONVICTION WAS OVERTURNED BECAUSE THE FEDERAL JUDGE PERCEIVED A FLAW IN THE INDICTMENT— NOT HIS MURDER CONVICTION.

ON OCTOBER 1ST, WHILE THE ORDER FOR HERMAN'S RELEASE WAS BEING IGNORED, ALBERT AND I OBTAINED PERMISSION TO VISIT HIM ONE LAST TIME.

HERMAN'S WAITING FOR US, ALBERT!

I GOT THE NEWS ON MY WAY TO THE PRISON.

HEY, MY BROTHER!

HERMAN, WE LOVE YOU, AND TODAY, YOU ARE GETTING OUT.

ALBERT? ROBERT? IS IT REALLY YOU?!

THAT DAY, WE FOUND OURSELVES TOGETHER ONE LAST TIME, AND ALBERT TOLD HIM THAT HE WAS FREE.

HERMAN PASSED AWAY ON OCTOBER 4TH, 2013.

ON FEBRUARY 19TH, 2016, ALBERT WOODFOX, THE LAST IMPRISONED MEMBER OF THE ANGOLA 3, WAS RELEASED AFTER MORE THAN FOUR DECADES IN SOLITARY CONFINEMENT.
THE FIGHT IS NOT OVER.

THE UNITED STATES ACCOUNTS FOR ONLY 5% OF THE WORLD'S POPULATION, BUT IS RESPONSIBLE FOR NEARLY 22% OF THE WORLD'S PRISON POPULATION. MORE THAN 2 MILLION PEOPLE ARE INCARCE- RATED IN U.S. PRISONS AS WELL AS LOCAL AND COUNTY JAILS.
1 IN 3 BLACK MEN IN THE UNITED STATES WILL GO TO PRISON OR JAIL IF CURRENT TRENDS CONTINUE.

THERE ARE 80,000 PRISONERS IN SOLITARY CONFINEMENT IN AMERICA EVERY DAY, DESPITE THE UNITED NATIONS COMMITTEE ON TORTURE'S DEMAND FOR REFORMS.

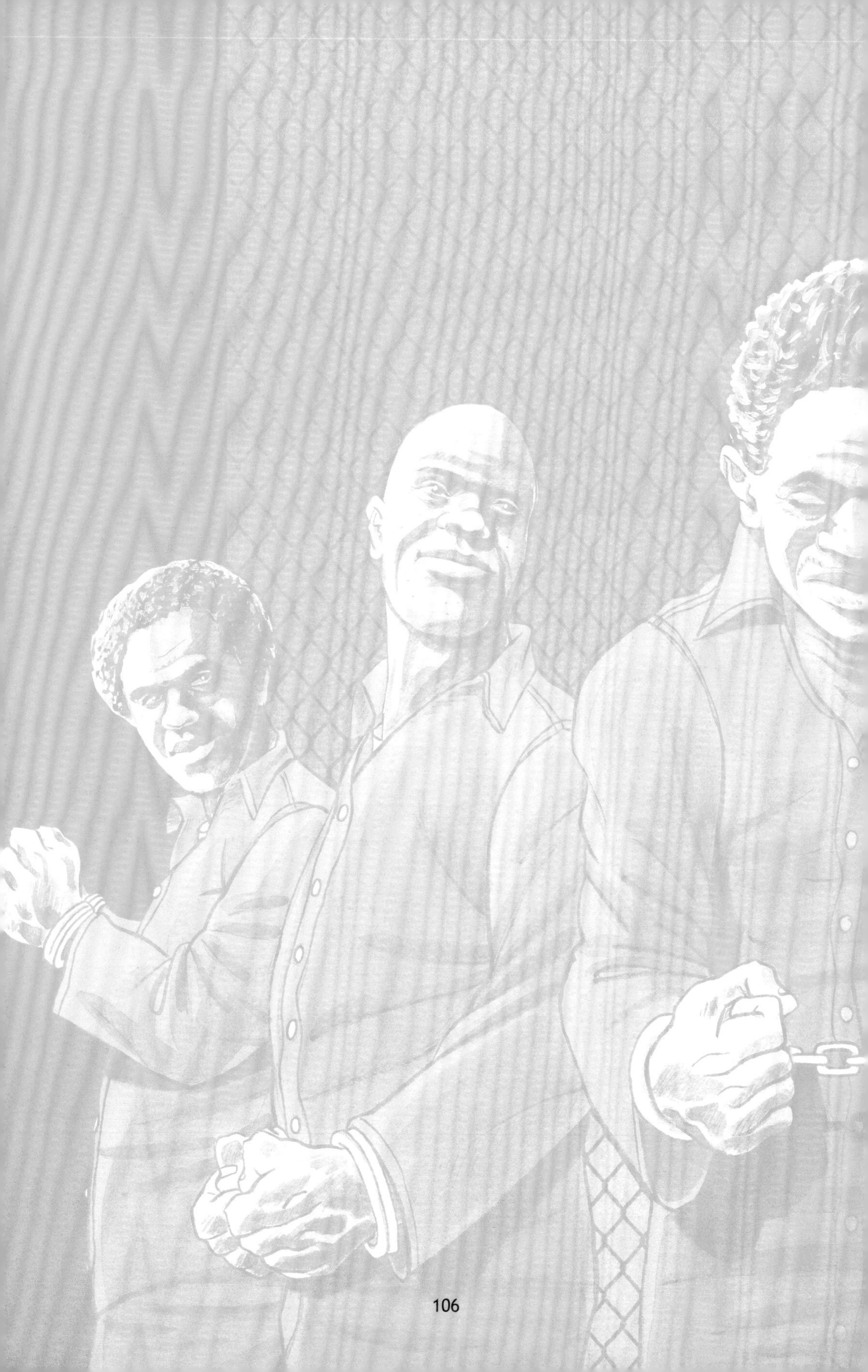

AN AFTERWORD BY ROBERT HILLARY KING

We were born in the USA, born Black, born poor. Is it any wonder that we spent most of our lives in prison?

My name is Robert H. King, the first freed member of the Angola 3. My comrades Albert Woodfox, Herman Wallace, and I were targeted for our activism as members of the Black Panther Party. After thirty-one years in Angola prison in Louisiana, twenty-nine spent in solitary confinement, I was released on February 8th, 2001. In 1970, a jury convicted me of a crime I did not commit and sentenced me to thirty-five years in prison. In 1972 I was brought to Angola State Penitentiary and placed under investigation for twenty-nine years for the murder of an Angola prison guard, even though I was 150 miles away at the time. Herman was released in October 2013 and tragically died two days later. I can now joyously report that Albert was released just months ago, on his birthday, February 19th, 2016. Albert and Herman were wrongly accused of this murder and convicted on the basis of a blind eyewitness and no physical evidence. We all ended up in CCR—close cell restriction—or solitary confinement—in a six-by-nine-foot cell. During this time we continued to organize prisoners to improve conditions and formed the first prison chapter of the Black Panther Party.

I may be free of Angola but Angola will never be free of me.

Since my release my life's focus has been to campaign against abuses of the criminal justice system—against the cruel and immoral legal system and against the torture of solitary confinement, as well as for the release of Albert and Herman. My comrade Herman passed away on October 1st, 2013, after just three days of freedom. Albert was released on February 19th, 2016, after forty-three years in solitary confinement.

I was in prison but prison was not in me.

The use of solitary confinement has been taken to a different level by the United States' industrial prison complex. People are put in a cell for twenty-three hours a day. The solitary confinement in the United States is the type that keeps you locked up twenty-three hours a day, sometimes twenty-four. That limits you, everywhere you go you're shackled and you're handcuffed. Sometimes you get punished for communicating, but guys communicated right along anyways. All "privileges" are minimized, as is human contact.

Legality and Morality are not bedfellows.

My personal evolution began in prison—in Angola State Penitentiary, in Louisiana—on an 18,000-acre former slave plantation. My experience in a six-by-nine-foot cell for twenty-nine years in solitary confinement taught me the difference between legality and morality.

The country where I was born—the United States of America—deifies the law and makes it holy. When we give legality this kind of God status we err. In the American political arena oftentimes politics is void of morality.

We have to continue to focus on the idea that just because something is legal doesn't mean that it is moral or that it is wholly correct. Legality and morality in the courthouse do not shake hands. There is an adversarial testing ground where the prosecuting attorney and defense attorney should meet.

When I say morality I am speaking of the morality that exists—the benevolence, the decency, that exists in human beings, the ability to be fair. And I am telling you that the legal system in the United States of America, and throughout the world, operates according to legal precepts. I don't have anything against legal precepts, but when legal precepts become a society's God, something is wrong. It was legal to own slaves during chattel slavery in America, but it wasn't until the people saw it as morally reprehensible that something was done about slavery. Prison is an extension of slavery. People say that the 13th Amendment abolished slavery, but nothing could be further from the truth. The 13th Amendment does not say slavery was a violation and just leave it at that. It goes on to say that slavery was abolished except for those who have been duly convicted of a crime. How many people in the States have been duly convicted

of a crime but are actually totally innocent? So if you are duly convicted of a crime—I mean legally sentenced for a crime—you can become a slave, and if you are legally sentenced to death they can kill you. They did it to Troy Davis. We all know he was legally incarcerated, but morally all of the evidence showed that he was actually innocent.

So I don't have anything against legal precepts if they are implemented according to morality, but if you just have a system based solely on legality, they can kill you. The system can kill you legally, but you will be morally innocent.

A case in point is the history of slavery in America. It was not until people began to see slavery as being reprehensible and amoral that it was abolished as we know it.

I realized that despite the fact that the 13th Amendment allegedly abolished slavery, slavery was never entirely abolished. I learned that a person could actually be innocent of a crime but convicted legally and that this person would be designated a legal slave—just as it was in 1864, when the constitution decreed that if you were Black being a slave was your lot. Modern day slavery is alive and well in America but it has taken on a different form—from the plantation to the prison.

We can make change happen—throw pebbles in a pond, you get ripples.

I am a firm believer in cause and effect. There is no doubt that people make a difference—public pressure from ordinary people from all around the world. I know that public pressure works and that public opinion matters. I have seen it at work in the courts. I have seen how it can make a difference in the decision making of those in the system with the power to determine a sentence, a verdict, or a judgment. I have also seen it at work in the media when they report on the stories that must be told, and further raise awareness of the case and wider issues.

Since my release I have seen the power of creativity and art coupled with an issue to move people to take action. I have traveled with artists such as Rigo 23 and Emory Douglas, the Black Panther Party's former Minister of Information. I have participated in mural projects from the last *quilombos* in Brazil, the ghettos in Portugal, from the streets of London to the townships of South Africa. Different art forms find new ways to address issues, to bring them to life and show the horror of human cruelty in a way people can digest.

This is why *Panthers in the Hole* is so important. My first experience of reading was reading cartoons. As a child they intrigued and motivated me and stimulated my desire to read more. In fact, now when I think about it, the images developed my perceptive skills and the words my conceptual skills. Without my knowing it, the combination of the pictures with words developed my cognitive thinking abilities. Reading was my lifeline in prison and I read so many books in prison I can't even recall! So this cartoon forms a critical part of the movement for change and the call for justice. I have no doubt that it will make a ripple in the pond…..

The struggle continues.

Knowing what I know, and knowing the illegal and inhumane torture that so many prisoners still endure every minute of every day on United States soil, the struggle for a more moral and just society endures. The fight for justice never ends. The fight to free all political prisoners past and present, as well as those prisoners who are currently in the system awaiting prosecution—victims of this unjust and discriminatory political system that is permeated by racism. This is their legacy and this is ours. Thank you for joining us.

All power to the people.

Robert Hillary King
June 2016

SOLITARY CONFINEMENT IN THE USA

(Information and statistics provided by Amnesty International)

The United States stands virtually alone in the world in incarcerating thousands of prisoners in long-term or indefinite solitary confinement, defined by the UN Special Rapporteur on Torture and other Cruel, Inhuman or Degrading Treatment or Punishment as "the physical and social isolation of individuals who are confined to their cells for 22 to 24 hours a day." More than 40 US states are believed to operate "super-maximum-security" units or prisons, collectively housing at least 25,000 prisoners. This number does not include the many thousands of other prisoners serving shorter periods in punishment or administrative segregation cells—estimated to be approximately 80,000 on any given day.

Amnesty International recognizes that the authorities have an obligation to ensure the safety of staff and inmates and that it may be necessary at times to segregate prisoners. However all measures must be consistent with the United States' obligation to treat all prisoners humanely, without exception. In recognition of the psychological harm that can result from isolating people even for relatively brief periods, international human rights experts and organizations have called on governments to restrict their use of solitary confinement so that it is applied only in exceptional circumstances, for the shortest possible period of time.

AN ESTIMATED 80,000 PRISONERS ARE HELD IN ISOLATION EVERY DAY.

THE FACTS ABOUT LOUISIANA STATE PENITENTIARY

Angola by the Numbers

There are 5,320 offenders held at the Louisiana State Penitentiary (Angola Prison). It is the largest maximum-security prison in the U.S.

Demographic Profile

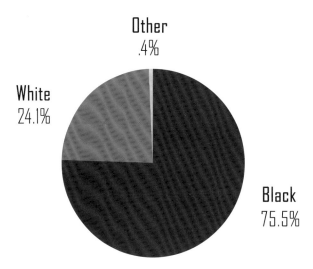

Other
.4%

White
24.1%

Black
75.5%

Inmate Profile

Average inmate age: 41.7 years old (with more than 1,000 inmates at Angola older than 55)

Average sentence: 12.6 years

Percentage serving a life sentence: 75.1%

Average time served: 55% have served, or are serving, 21 or more years; 23.9% less than a year to five years; 21.1% 11-15 years

Percentage imprisoned for violent crimes: 90.9%

Number on Death Row: 85, or 1.6% of the population[1]

1. Le Blanc, James M. "Demographic Profiles of Adult Offenders in Louisiana State Penitentiary." Louisiana Department of Public Safety and Corrections. 30 April 2015.

LOUISIANA HAS THE HIGHEST INCARCERATION RATE IN THE UNITED STATES, WITH 1 OUT OF EVERY 55 ADULTS BEHIND BARS.

As of March 2015, there were 37,615 total adult offenders incarcerated in the state of Louisiana, equating to .48% of the population.

The population is overwhelmingly male, at 94.4%, and primarily black, at 67.8% of the prisoner population. The racial breakdown of the prison population is the inverse of the state population.

4,923 individuals, or 13.1% of the prison population, are serving sentences of life without parole. Louisiana is the only state where that amount is more than 10%[2]. As of April 2015, 85 individuals are on death row.

Additionally, there are 70,728 adults on parole, probation, or under goodtime/parole supervision. Individuals who were incarcerated for drug related offenses were released on parole at the highest rate, amounting to 45.6% of inmates who receive parole. In Louisiana, all life sentences are without parole.

To learn more about what you can do to bring about prison reform, visit amnestyusa.org

---

2. Le Blanc, James M. "Demographic Profiles of Adult Probation and Parole Population." Louisiana Department of Public Safety and Corrections. 31 Mar. 2015.